PEARL
BUYING GUIDE

Above: Chinese freshwater pearl necklace with an iolite enhancer set with a ruby, diamond, and Chinese freshwater pearls and featuring a large American freshwater pearl. *Necklace and enhancer designed and crafted by Anita Selinger; photo by Ralph Gabriner.*

Opposite page: South Sea, Tahitian and Chinese freshwater cultured pearls from Sea Hunt Pearls. *Photo by Lee-Carraher.*

PEARL
BUYING GUIDE

How to Identify and Evaluate Pearls & Pearl Jewelry

5th Edition

Renée Newman

 International Jewelry Publications
Los Angeles _____

First published 1992
Second Edition 1994
Reprinted 1996
Third Edition 1999
Reprinted 2001
Fourth Edition 2004
Reprinted 2005

International Jewelry Publications
P.O. Box 13384
Los Angeles, CA 90013-0384 USA

(Inquiries should be accompanied by a self-addressed, stamped envelope.)

Printed in Singapore

Library of Congress Cataloging-in-Publication Data

Newman, Renée.
    Pearl buying guide: how to identify and evaluate pearls & pearl jewelry / Renée Newman – 5th ed.
            p.   cm.
    Includes bibliographical references and index.
    ISBN 978-0-929975-44-3 (alk. paper)
1. Pearls--Purchasing.   I. Title.
    TS755.P3N49 2010
    639'.412--dc22

                                                                2009050550

Front Cover photos:
South Sea Pearls and photo from King Plutarco Inc.
Tahitian pearl earrings from A & Z Pearls; *photo by Diamond Graphics.*
Spine: Cortez Pearl™ and photo from Columbia Gem House.
Back cover: Tahitian pearl ring from Divina Pearls. *Photo by Cristina Gregory.*

Contents

Acknowledgments

I would like to express my appreciation to the following people for their contribution to the *Pearl Buying Guide*:

Ernie and Regina Goldberger of the Josam Diamond Trading Corporation. This book could never have been written without the experience and knowledge I gained from working with them. Some of the pearls pictured in this book are or were part of their collection.

Eve Alfillé, Francisco Adame, Albert Asher, Blaire Beavers, KC. Bell, Charles Carmona, Pin P. Chen, Shane Elan, Patricia Esparza, Susan B. Johnson, Betty Sue King, Chien Lin, Peter Malnekoff, Henri Masliah, Rick Matsui, Lynn Marie Nakamura, Wes & Tish Rankin, Avi Raz, Jet Taylor, Charles Ueng, and Fuji Voll. They have made valuable suggestions, corrections and comments regarding the portions of the book they examined. They are not responsible for any possible errors, nor do they necessarily endorse the material contained in this book.

A & Z Pearls, Inc., Adachi America, Inc., Albert Cohen Co., Blue River Gems & Jewelry Co., Bonhams & Butterfield, Eliko Pearl, Gladys Evans, Grace Pearl Co., Inter World Trading, Jye's International, Inc., King Plutarco, Inc., Kojima Company, Stephen Metzler, Overland Gems, Inc., Pacific Coast Pearls, Pacific Pearls, Paspaley Pearling Co. Pty. Ltd. Shima Pearl Company, Inc., Timeless Gem Designs, Marge Vaughn, Yokoo Pearls and Roslyn Zalenka. Their pearls or clasps have been used for some of the photographs.

A & Z Pearls, Albert Asher South Sea Pearl Co., Eve J. Alfillé Gallery, American Pearl Co, Assael International Inc., K. C. Bell Natural Pearls, Blair Beavers, Barbara Berk, Busatti, Columbia Gem House, Angela Conty, Erica Courtney, Paula Crevoshay, Cultured Pearl Association of America, Gary Dulac, Divina Pearls, Gem A, Gemological Institute of America, GAAJ Research Lab, Eittige, Galatea, Hikari South Sea Pearl Co, Inc, Inter World Trading, Japan Pearl Exporters' Association, Jewels by Woods, Sandy Jones, King Plutarco, King's Ransom, Kojima Company, Latendresse family, Gail Levine, Mikimoto (America) Co. Inc, Moana Natural Pearl Co, Pala International, Pearl Exporting Co, Pearl Paradise, Linda K. Quinn Designs, Rain Forest Designs, King's Ransom, Krespi & White, Pacific Coast Pearls, Pacific Pearls, Pearce Design, Pearl Concepts King Plutarco, earl Society Collection, Pearlworkds, Michael Saldivar, Anita Selinger, Mark Schneider Design, Sea Hunt Pearls, Shogun Pearl Co, Skinny Dog Design Group, SSEF Swiss Gemmological Institute, T. Stern, Trigem Designs, Gabriele Weinmann, and Zaffiro. Photos or diagrams from them have been reproduced in this book.

Frank Chen, Gladys Chong, Ion Itescu, Dawn King, Joyce Ng, and Monique Truchet. They have provided technical assistance.

Louise Harris Berlin, editor of the *Pearl Buying Guide*. Thanks to her, this book is much easier for consumers to read and understand.

My sincere thanks to all of these contributors for their kindness and help.

1

Curious Facts about Pearls

The pearl is the oldest known gem, and for centuries it was considered the most valuable. To the ancients, pearls were a symbol of the moon and had magical powers which could bring prosperity and long life. In Indian mythology, pearls were heavenly dewdrops that fell into the sea and were caught by shellfish.

Throughout history, pearls have been considered divine gifts especially suited for royalty. Women who wanted to gain the favor of a king would offer him pearls. In Persia, crowns with double circlets of pearls were the symbol of royal and divine birth. This became a custom elsewhere as well. When Julius Caesar became emperor of the Roman Empire, he claimed descent from the gods and was crowned with a pearl diadem.

Pearls have also been considered ideal wedding gifts because they symbolize purity and innocence. In the Hindu religion, the presentation of an undrilled pearl and its piercing has formed part of the marriage ceremony.

Some cultures, such as the Chinese, have used pearls medically to cure a variety of ailments, including indigestion and heart disease. Pearls have also been prescribed as a love potion and tonic for long life. Today, the main component of pearls, calcium carbonate ($CaCO_3$), is used as an antacid and a dietary supplement. Calcium manganese carbonate is an important heart medicine. At the age of 94, Mikimoto, founder of the cultured pearl industry stated, "I owe my fine health and long life to the two pearls I have swallowed every morning of my life since I was twenty."

Pearls are found in saltwater oysters and freshwater mussels. If they are **natural,** they are usually formed as the mollusk secretes layers of a protective, pearly substance called **nacre** (pronounced NAY-ker) around an irritant. This irritant, which accidentally enters the mollusk, can be a minute snail, worm, fish or crab, or particle of shell, clay or mud, and is called a **nucleus.** Experimentation and pearl slicing, however, have led some pearl researchers to believe that most natural round pearls are caused by the accidental entry of a parasitic worm into a mollusk.

When pearls are **cultured**, the irritant is intentionally introduced by man. In the case of most freshwater pearls, pieces of mantle (a membranous tissue that secretes nacre and lines the inner shell surface of mollusks) are inserted into a mussel. Saltwater cultured pearls, however, usually originate from the insertion of a shell bead nucleus along with a bit of oyster mantle tissue into an oyster. These are called **bead nucleated pearls.** Freshwater pearls may also be bead nucleated. The shape and size of the resulting pearls depend to a large degree on the shape and size of the implanted irritant. The choice of mantle tissue can also affect the color of the pearl.

Saltwater oysters usually produce only one pearl per harvest. Afterwards, the oyster can be renucleated one or two more times. However, with each successive implantation, the quality of the resulting pearl usually decreases. Freshwater mussels can produce as many as 30 to 50 pearls, per harvest, which is one reason freshwater pearls typically cost less than saltwater pearls of similar quality.

Fig. 1.1 Chinese freshwater pearl farm. The empty capped green soda bottles are used as flares.

Fig. 1.2 Farmers usually store three mussels per net pouch during the three- to seven- year growth period.

Fig. 1.3 Pearl farmer with a mussel from the above Grace Pearl farm.

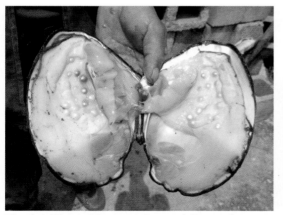

Fig. 1.4. View of the opened mussel. It contains more than 30 pearls of various colors and sizes.

Fig. 1.5 Pearls from mussel above.

Above photos © Renée Newman

Fig. 1.6 Pearls in a bleaching solution. The metal container keeps them warm at a specified temperature.

Fig. 1.7 Light helps whiten the pearls, but bleaching solution is also required.

Fig. 1.8 Washing pearls after bleaching

Fig. 1.9 Drying the pearls after washing

Fig. 1.10 Hyriopsis cumingii shells

Fig. 1.11 Shell with Beijing 2008 Olympic emblem

All photos of the Grace Pearl factory on this page © Renée Newman

Fig. 1.13 A Japanese polishing machine used for large quantities of pearls

Fig. 1.12 A typical polishing machine in China

Fig. 1.14 Pearl sorting room

Fig. 1.15 Sorting pearls for quality

Fig. 1.16 Selecting quality & stringing pearls

Fig. 1.17 Bags of pearls ready for sale

All photos of the Grace Pearl factory on this page © Renée Newman

Fig. 1.18 South-Sea Pearl farm in Indonesia. *Photo from the Hikari South Sea Pearl Co.*

Left: **Fig 1.19**. Net panel containing oysters with inserted nuclei. Nets are suspended about 3 to 6 meters below the water surface for a cultivation period of about two years.

Below: **Fig 1.20** Insertion of a shell-bead nucleus into a South Sea pearl oyster. *Both photos courtesy Hikari South Sea Pearl Co.*

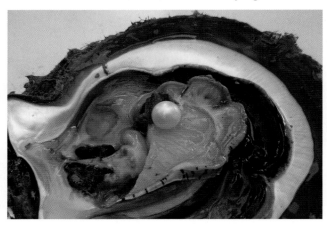

Fig. 1.21 Cultured pearl in a freshly opened South Sea oyster from Paspaley Pearling Co. Pty. Ltd. *Photo © Blaire Beavers.*

The first major sources of pearls were the Persian Gulf and the Gulf of Mannar between India and Sri Lanka. The Talmud, Bible, Koran and Indian texts mention pearls from these areas. More detailed accounts of pearl exploration were provided after the 15th century when Christopher Columbus and Vasco de Balboa discovered pearls in Venezuela and Panama.

Until the development of the gold and silver mines in Mexico and Peru, pearls were the New World's biggest export. In fact, the value of pearls exceeded that of all other exports combined; and in Spain, the Americas became known as "The Lands that Pearls Come From." One of the most famous pearls *La Peregrina* ("The Incomparable"), was found in the Americas. A pear-shaped pearl about the size of a pigeon's egg, *La Peregrina* is particularly noted for its beauty. Among its owners have been Philip II of Spain, Mary Tudor of England, Napoleon III and Elizabeth Taylor. According to one story, the slave diver that found it was rewarded with his freedom and his master with a plot of land and a position as mayor.

Nowadays the number of oysters producing natural pearls around Venezuela and Panama is insignificant. One reminder of what an important source of pearls this area once was is the name of an island off the Venezuelan coast, the Isle of Margarita. "Margarita" means pearls. Incidentally, if your name is Margaret, Peggy, Marjorie, Margot, Maggie, Gretchen, Gretel or Rita, it also means "pearl," which in turn signifies purity, innocence, humility and sweetness.

Overfishing has also occurred in n the Middle East, North America, Asia, and in parts of Europe. As a result the production of natural pearls has either disappeared or been drastically reduced in these areas. They've been replaced by cultured pearls, which share the unique qualities of natural pearls. These were particularly well described by George Kunz and Charles Stevenson in 1908 in the *Book of the Pearl*.

Unlike other gems, the pearl comes to us perfect and beautiful, direct from the hand of nature. Other precious stones receive careful treatment from the lapidary, and owe much to his art. The pearl, however, owes nothing to man . . . It is absolutely a gift of nature, on which man cannot improve. We turn from the brilliant, dazzling ornament of diamonds or emeralds to a necklace of pearls with a sense of relief, and the eye rests upon it with quiet, satisfied repose and is delighted with its modest splendor, its soft gleam, borrowed from its home in the depths of the sea. It seems truly to typify steady and abiding affection, which needs no accessory or adornment to make it more attractive. And there is a purity and sweetness about it which makes it especially suitable for the maiden.

2
Pearl Price Factors in a Nutshell

The following factors can affect the price of pearls:

Luster
Surface quality
Shape
Color
Size
Nacre (pearl coating) thickness and quality
Matching
Treatment status (untreated or treated? type of treatment)
Pearl type (saltwater/freshwater, natural/cultured, whole/blister)

LUSTER: Pearl brilliance; the shine and glow of a pearl. The greater and deeper the luster, the more valuable the pearl. Pearls with a high luster display strong and sharp light reflections and a good contrast between the bright and darker areas of the pearl. Pearls with low luster look milky, chalky and dull. Select pearls that have a good luster. For more information, see Chapter 5.

SURFACE QUALITY: The fewer and smaller the flaws, the more valuable the pearl. Blemishes on single pearls tend to be more obvious and less acceptable than those on strands. It's normal for pearl strands to have some flaws. Natural pearls and cultured pearls from the South Seas are more likely to have flaws than Japanese Akoyas. Additional photos and details are provided in Chapter 7.

SHAPE: Normally, the more round and symmetrical the pearl, the more it costs. Unique, asymmetrical shapes, however, are also desirable, and are used to create distinctive pearl pieces. The lowest priced shapes are baroque (irregular and asymmetrical in shape) or have ring-like formations encircling the pearl.

COLOR: Saltwater pearls that are yellowish usually sell for less than those which are white or light pink. Golden South Sea pearls from Indonesia and the Philippines are an exception and can sell for as much as white South Sea pearls, provided the gold color is intense and natural.

Natural-color black pearls (they're actually gray) can sell for as much as white pearls of the same size and quality, as long as they have overtone colors and are not just plain gray. The overtone colors, which are visible in the light-colored areas of black pearls, may be green, pink, blue or purple.

Pink overtones are desirable on white pearls and are visible in the dark areas of the pearl. Greenish or yellowish overtones tend to reduce the price of white pearls. Occasionally, iridescent rainbow-like colors are visible on pearls. Pearl iridescence is always considered a valuable quality.

Luster qualities ranging
from high to very low

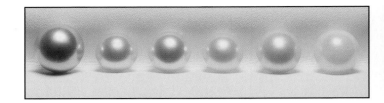

Surface qualities ranging
from clean to
heavily blemished

Some South Sea pearl shapes:
round, oval, drop, button,
circled drop, baroque

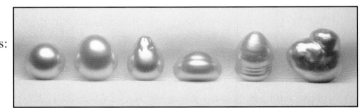

Some Australian South Sea
pearl colors

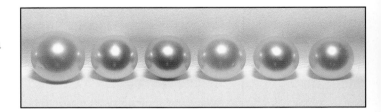

Some Indonesian South Sea
pearl colors

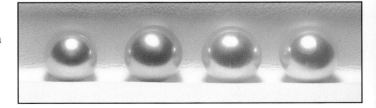

Some Tahitian pearl colors

*Pearls this page courtesy
King Plutarco, Inc.
Photos © Renée Newman*

The way in which color affects the pricing of freshwater pearls varies from one dealer to another. Often it has little or no effect. However, when comparing the prices of any pearls, try to compare pearls of the same type and color.

SIZE: Usually the larger the pearl, the more it costs, depending on availability.

NACRE THICKNESS: Nacre (NAY-ker) thickness is not a price factor for natural pearls because they're nearly all nacre (a pearly substance that mollusks secrete around irritants). However, it's of critical importance in cultured saltwater pearls. See Chapter 4. (**Natural pearls** are formed around an irritant such as a shell particle or parasite that accidentally enters a mollusk. **Cultured pearls** are formed after a human intentionally inserts a shell bead nucleus and/or a piece of oyster or mussel tissue in a mollusk. If the bead nucleus isn't left in the mollusk long enough, the mollusk won't have time to coat it with enough microscopic layers of nacre to make a lustrous pearl).

The thicker the nacre coating of a pearl, the better and more durable the pearl. South Sea pearls normally have a thicker nacre coating than Akoya pearls. Nacre thickness is one of the most important quality factors for cultured saltwater pearls because it affects both pearl beauty and durability.

Nacre thickness is not as important a factor in cultured freshwater pearls as it is in saltwater pearls. This is because most freshwater pearls have no shell nucleus. When one is present, the nacre is usually thicker than in Akoya pearls.

MATCHING: The better pearls blend together in terms of color, shape, luster, size and surface quality, the more valuable they are. Finding well-matched, high quality pearls can be a challenge.

TREATMENT STATUS: Dyed and irradiated pearls cost less than those of natural color and affect the price more than bleaching. During the 1920's and 30's, however, dyed black pearls were considered fashionable and sometimes sold for as much as white pearls of similar size and quality. Other kinds of treatments and tests for detecting dyed pearls are discussed in Chapter 13.

PEARL TYPE: Before you price a pearl, you should know, for example, if it's **saltwater** (from the oceans, sea, gulf or bay) or if it's **freshwater** (from a river, lake or pond). Good saltwater pearls (e.g., South Sea and Japanese Akoya) can cost several times more than freshwater pearls of similar quality and size. One of the reasons for this is that one mussel in a lake can produce as many as forty freshwater pearls in one harvest. An oyster in the sea typically produces one or sometimes two saltwater pearls at a time. It should be noted, however, that some strands of large round pink freshwater pearls have retailed for more than $10,000.

Natural pearls are more valuable than cultured pearls. Chapter 15 explains how to distinguish cultured pearls from those that are natural.

Whole pearls are much more valued than **blister pearls**—those which grow attached to the inner surface of a mollusk shell and **three-quarter pearls**—whole pearls that have been ground or sawed on one side, usually to remove blemishes. **Mabe pearls** are made from blister pearls by removing the interior, filling it with a paste and covering it with a mother of pearl backing. These assembled pearls offer a big look at a low price, but they're not as durable as non assembled pearls, which are higher priced. See Chapter 3 for photos and more information.

3

Pearl Types

When you think of a pearl, what's the first shape and color that come to your mind? Perhaps round and white. But if you lived in Tahiti, you might initially think of a dark grayish pearl and it wouldn't necessarily be round. Pearls come in a wide range of shapes, types and colors; in this chapter we'll define the various types and explain the role that pearl type plays in determining the value of a pearl.

Pearl Types

The difference between natural and cultured pearls was explained in Chapter 1. Technically the term **pearl** should only refer to a natural pearl. Nevertheless, cultured pearls are so common now and natural ones so rare that "pearl" normally refers to a cultured pearl (One exception is in certain Arab countries where cultured pearls tend to be frowned upon. Pearls there are generally considered a special gift from God that should be entirely a product of nature.) For the sake of brevity, in this book, cultured pearls will often be labeled as "pearls." When shopping for pearls, you may come across the term **semi-cultured**. It refers to imitation pearls. Many members of the trade consider it a deceptive term designed to trick buyers into thinking they are getting cultured pearls when they aren't.

Additionally, pearls can be classified as saltwater or freshwater. People tend to be most familiar with **saltwater pearls**, which come from oysters in oceans, seas, gulfs and bays. The best-known example is the Akoya pearl shown in figure 3.1 and discussed on the next page.

Fig. 3.1 Cultured Akoya pearls from Sea Hunt Pearls. *Photo by Lee-Carraher.*

Freshwater pearls (fig. 3.3) are found in mussels or oysters in rivers, lakes or ponds and tend to be more irregular in shape and more varied in color than pearls found in saltwater oysters. Chapter 12 provides more information on freshwater pearls. Pearls are further classified into the categories below:

Oriental Pearls: Natural pearls found in oysters of the Persian Gulf or those that look like pearls found there (according to the USA Federal Trade Commission). Sometimes this term is used to designate either any natural saltwater pearl or more specifically, any natural saltwater pearl found in the West Asia Area, e.g., in the Red Sea, the Persian Gulf or the Gulf of Mannar off the west coast of Sri Lanka.

A more precise definition of "Oriental pearl" is given by the respected pearl researcher, Koji Wada, in *Pearls of the World* (pg. 69): He says "[Oriental pearls are] natural pearls from one kind of sea-water pearl oyster called the wing shell."

Akoya Pearls: Saltwater pearls from the Akoya oyster (*Pinctada fucata martensii*), which are usually cultured (fig. 3.1). These pearls are typically roundish, and their natural body colors normally range from light pink, to white, to yellowish. The chapters on pearl quality in this book focus on Akoya pearls. Even though they are often called Japanese pearls, they can also be found in oysters outside Japan. In fact, China has become the major producer of Akoya pearls. Korea, Vietnam, Hong Kong and Sri Lanka also culture pearls using the Akoya oyster.

South Sea Pearls: Used sometimes as a general term signifying any saltwater pearl found in the area extending from the Philippines and Indonesia down to Australia and across to French Polynesia (fig 3.2). More often than not, it refers specifically to large white or yellow pearls cultured in the *Pinctada maxima* oyster—a large oyster found in the South Seas, also called the silver-lip or yellow-lip (also gold-lip) oyster depending on the color of its shell lip.

South Sea pearls tend to range from 9–19 mm, whereas Akoya pearls usually range from 1–10 mm. You can read more about South Sea pearls in Chapter 10.

Black Pearls: Pearls of natural color (not dyed) from the black-lip (*Pinctada margaritifera*) oyster in the Western to Central Pacific Ocean or from the La Paz pearl oyster (Pinctada mazatlanica) or rainbow-lipped oyster (*Pteria sterna*) in the Eastern Pacific between Baja California and Peru. Some people use the term "black pearl" to refer to any dark colored pearl, whether it is dyed or natural in color. (See Chapter 11.) Black pearls from French Polynesia are often called **Tahitian pearls**.

Biwa Pearls: Freshwater pearls cultivated in Lake Biwa, Japan's largest lake. Sometimes other freshwater cultured pearls are called Biwas in order to impress buyers. Lake Biwa was one of the first freshwater culturing sites and it has been noted for its high quality pearls. Because of pollution, however, production has been greatly reduced.

Kasumiga™: Pearls named after Lake Kasumigara, north of Tokyo, where they are cultured in *Hyriopsis schlegelii x Hyriopsis cumingii* hybrid mussels. Kasumiga™ pearls, which have also been generically called Kasumi pearls, were introduced to the market in the mid 1990's and are only available in limited quantities. These nucleated freshwater pearls range in size from 11–16 mm and in color from purple to pink to white to gold. See figures 3.5 and 3.10.

Blue Pearls: Dark-colored pearls found in oysters such as the Akoya or silver-lip oysters. The color is caused by foreign contaminants in the nacre or between the nacre and shell bead nucleus unlike black pearls whose color is an inherent characteristic of the pearl nacre. (Hisada and Komatsu, *Pearls of the World*, page 88 and Robert Webster, *Gems*, page 506).

Half Pearls: "Whole pearls that have been ground or sawed on one side, usually to remove blemishes" (as defined in The GIA *Jeweler's Manual*). If the sawed pearl looks too large to be a half pearl, it's called a **three-quarter pearl** (fig. 3.8).

Fig. 3.2 White, golden and black South Sea pearls from A & Z Pearls. *Photo by Diamond Graphics.*

Fig. 3.3 Freshwater pearls from Pacific Pearls, who describe their unique brown-green-goldy natural color as "pond-slime color." *Photo by Marcia Fentress.*

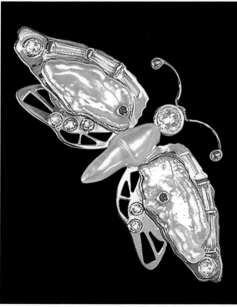

Fig. 3.4 Biwa-like freshwater pearl pin. *Design copyright by Eve J. Alfillé; photo by Matthew Arden.*

Fig. 3.6 Whole black and white South Sea pearls with an Acorn shape. They resemble 3/4 pearls when mounted in this brooch. *Photo and jewelry from Albert Asher South Sea Pearl Co.*

Fig. 3.5 Kasumi pearl bracelet. *Design copyright by Eve J. Alfillé; photo by Matthew Arden.*

Fig. 3.8 A 3/4 pearl which could look like a whole pearl in a closed back setting. *Photo © Renée Newman.*

Fig. 3.7 South Sea and Akoya mabe pearls from King Plutarco Co. *Photo © Renée Newman.*

Fig. 3.9 Mabe pearls with a nacre rim. "Blister mabe pearls." *Photo © Renée Newman.*

Fig. 3.10 Kasumi drops. *Design © Eve Alfillé; photo: Matthew Arden.*

Natural half pearls were often used in Victorian jewelry. They were usually made by cutting off the best parts from large irregular pearls. Half and three-quarter pearls are priced lower than whole pearls of the same shape and quality. Button- and acorn-shaped South-Sea pearls have a flattened side which can make them look like half or three-quarter pearls when mounted (fig. 3.6). The term "half pearl" is sometimes used to refer to blister pearls.

Blister Pearls: Natural or cultured pearls that grow attached to the inner surface of the oyster or mussel shell. When cut from the shell, one side is left flat with no pearly coating. Some people apply the term "blister" only to natural pearls of this type. Cultured blister pearls are not new. As far back as the 13th century, the Chinese were placing small lead images of the sitting Buddha inside freshwater mussels against their shells. The resulting pearly buddhas were either removed and sold as good-luck charms or else left attached to the shell and used as an ornamental curiosity.

Tennessee is a major source of cultured solid blister pearls. These American blister pearls come in a variety of shapes and are marketed under the name of domé® (fig 3.11). Their nacre is thicker than that of mabe pearls, making them more durable.

Mabe Pearls: Assembled cultured blister pearls (fig. 3.7) (pronounced MAH-bay). The blister pearl is cultured by gluing against the inside of the shell a half-bead nucleus (often of plastic or soapstone). After the mollusk has secreted nacre over the bead, the blister pearl is cut from the shell; and the bead is removed so the pearl can be cleaned to prevent deterioration. The remaining hole is filled with a paste or wax (and sometimes also a bead) and then covered with a mother-of-pearl backing. Mabe pearls are not as not as durable as solid blister pearls.

It can be hard to distinguish between mabe, blister or half pearls when they are mounted in jewelry. As a consequence, these three terms often end up being used interchangeably.

Despite all the work involved in assembling mabe pearls, they are relatively inexpensive for their large size. This is partly because several can be grown in one oyster and because they are grown in oysters that have rejected a whole nucleus or that are judged unsuitable for producing whole pearls. Also, any type of half pearl will cost far less than if it were whole, no matter what type of oyster it is grown in.

Most large mabe assembled pearls come from the silver-lip or black-lip oysters, but technically the term "mabe" should refer only to pearls cultivated in mabe oysters (*Pteria penguin*). The true **mabe-oyster pearls** are known for having a better luster, color and iridescence than pearls cultured in other oysters and are, consequently, more valuable. Most of those harvested are half or three-quarter blister pearls. If a salesperson claims that the jewelry you are buying is made with a mabe-oyster pearl, have him or her write this on the receipt. It's helpful for insurance and appraisal purposes. Information on the cultur-ing of mabe oysters can be found in a write-up by Morimitsu Muramatsu in *Pearls of the World* (pp. 79 to 86).

Mabe Blister Pearls: An informal term used by some dealers to designate mabe pearls with a rim, making them resemble a fried egg (fig. 3.9). The term "blister mabe" is also used. Technically, though, all assembled mabe pearls originate as blister pearls and after they are assembled, they are mabe pearls with a rim.

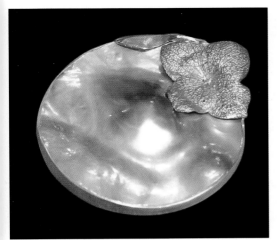

Fig. 3.11 Cultured domé® pearl from Tennessee. *Design © Eve Alfillé; photo by Matthew Arden.*

Fig. 3.12 Cultured Cortez™ pearl (9-10 mm). *Ring and photo from Trigem Designs.*

Fig. 3.13 Saltwater keshi pearls. *Pearls and photo from the Pearl Exporting Company.*

Fig. 3.14 Natural rainbow pearls (black pearls from the *Pteria sterna* oyster). *Pearls/photo: Pacific Coast Pearls.*

Rainbow Pearls: A trade name for pearls from the Western winged (rainbow-lipped) pearl oyster (*Pteria sterna*), which is noted for its high luster and rainbow-like colors.

This rainbow lipped oyster ranges naturally off the eastern Pacific Coast from California to Peru. Some are cultivated as mabe and whole pearls near Guaymas, Mexico. "Rainbow pearls," which are generically called "black pearls," are found in a variety of colors: lavender, pink, red, blue, green, purple, silver, gold, black and brown, with varying shades and combinations. It's not unusual to see three or four color variations on one pearl.

Black pearls were discovered in 1533, when Spanish captain Fortún Jiménez became the first European known to have landed in Baja California. For the next 300 years, natural black pearls from the rainbow-lipped oyster and the La Paz pearl oyster (Pinctada mazatlanica) were an important export.

Unfortunately, the construction of the Hoover Dam depleted nutrients in the Gulf of California, diminishing natural pearl production in the area. To protect the oysters, the government banned harvesting of natural oyster beds in 1939. The Monterrey Technical Institute in Guaymas began studying pearl culturing in 1993, and produced the first experimental round pearls in 1996.

Whole cultured rainbow pearls range from seven to about 12 mm in diameter and have a good nacre thickness. Their natural counterparts are found in sizes from seed to 30-carat pearls and range in price from $100 per carat to $2000 per carat wholesale. Cultured rainbow pearls cost less, with mabes being the least expensive.

Cortez Pearls™: A trade name for dark saltwater pearls from the rainbow-lipped (*Pteria sterna*) oyster that are cultured by Columbia Gem House, Inc. in Bacochibampo Bay in the Sea of Cortez near the city of Guaymas, Mexico. These pearls are available in semi-round, drop and round shapes. Cortez pearls are too rare to be used for strands. They retail from $75 to $300 for fine baroque shapes. Pear shapes and rounds are $200 to $750. Rare large exceptional Cortez pearls can command $2,000 each.

Cultured Cortez Pearls can be distinguished from cultured Tahitian pearls, which many closely resemble, by their distinctive red fluorescence under long-wave ultraviolet light. Cortez Pearls also show a greater range of iridescent colors, including some shades that are not exhibited by black pearls from other areas of the world.

Seed Pearls: Tiny, natural pearls that measure less than two millimeters. They usually weigh less than 0.06 carats.

Keshi: A general term used by pearl traders for pearls that grow accidentally in the soft tissue or the adductor muscle of cultured pearl-bearing mollusks. Chien Lin, president of Inter World Trading, says that the term "keshi" started out referring to a type of natural pearl in Japan, but over time the term became much more broadly used internationally. Having grown up in the pearl industry in Kobe, Japan, Lin had the opportunity to meet many old-generation pearl traders. They told him the term "keshi" was initially used to refer to natural seed pearls found when harvesting wild Akoya oysters. Since the tiny natural pearls resembled poppy seeds, they called them *keshi*, which means "poppy" in Japanese. Lin has verified this usage of the term with a specialist at the Mikimoto Pearl Museum in Japan.

Fig. 3.16 Large Tahitian keshi. *Pearls and photo from Hikari South Sea Pearl Company.*

Left: Fig. 3.15 South Seas keshi pearl necklace with a South Seas baroque pearl drop. *Necklace by Zaffiro. Photo by Elizabeth Gualtieri.*

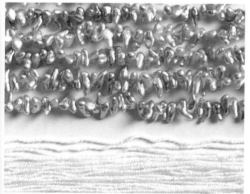

Fig. 3.17 Size ranges of Akoya keshi (actual size). *Pearls and photo from Inter World Trading.*

Fig. 3.18 Freshwater keshi (bottom) and "reborn pearls" (top), actual size. *From Inter World Trading.*

After the Japanese started culturing Akoya pearls, the term "keshi" was also used for the by-products of Akoya cultivation that did not contain a bead nucleus. These form from nacre secretion around microorganisms or shell particles that enter the pearl during pearl nucleation. The nacre may also be secreted around detached fragments of the mantle inserted with the pearl nuclei (mantle is a membranous tissue that secretes nacre and lines the inner shell surface of mollusks. It's inserted with the pearl bead nucleus to help stimulate nacre formation). Mantle tissue keshi have also been called "saibo (tissue) keshi," but most traders just call them keshi. Akoya keshi pearls can range from small "seed-sized" to skinny pearls as long as 14 mm.

The term became more confusing when freshwater pearls and South Sea pearls from the silver- and black-lipped oysters entered the market. Keshi from South Sea pearl oysters are generally much larger in size than Akoya pearls because of the size of the mother of pearl and speed of the nacre formation.

Even though South Sea keshi seldom look like poppy seeds or tiny pearls, the term "keshi" is used to refer to these by-products of South Sea oysters. There is a large range of sizes for South Sea keshi—from small seed-sized to the size of a baby's fist.

To add another element of confusion to the term "keshi," Chinese reborn freshwater pearls (*Zai Sheng Zhu* in Mandarin) came into the picture. A **reborn pearl** is grown out of the pearl sack of a mussel in which a pearl was carefully removed at harvest so as to not kill the mussel. Another pearl will grow out of a pearl sack, after healing, without another implantation of a mantle or tissue. (This tissue is originally necessary to initiate the virgin grafting to stimulate pearl nacre formation). Some people call these **"born again" pearls** or **second generation pearls.**

Freshwater reborn pearls are not new to the market. This category of pearls had been available from Biwa Lake pearl farms in Japan when Biwa pearls were still in production. (Actual pearl cultivation in Biwa Lake faded out in the late 1980's, leaving very few farmers still cultivating on a small scale). At that time, Biwa pearl traders did not use the term "keshi" for reborn pearls; they simply called them "Biwa pearls," the general term for freshwater pearls produced at Biwa Lake.

Some traders refer to Chinese reborn pearls as "natural pearls" or "Biwa pearls," but both terms are wrongfully used. Reborn pearls are not natural pearls because they are cultivated, and "Biwa pearl" is a general term for freshwater pearls out of Biwa Lake in Japan. Most of the Chinese freshwater pearl cultivation techniques came from Japanese pearl farmers, so too the South Sea pearl cultivation techniques of the black- and silver/gold-lipped pearl oysters.

Chien Lin prefers to refer to these reborn pearls as "keshi-type cultured freshwater pearls" because the nature of the reborn pearls is different from that of other keshi pearls. Reborn pearls are intentionally created while keshi pearls are created by accident.

Japanese Akoya keshi are becoming more and more difficult to find because of recent decreases in Japanese Akoya pearl production, but some other types of keshi are becoming more available due to the increase in overall production of freshwater pearls and black, white and yellow South Sea pearls. Akoya keshi are sent for processing to countries with low labor costs because the majority of Akoya keshi are very small or thin and thus have smaller-than-usual holes that must be drilled by hand without using any power tools.

In summary the term "keshi" has been used to refer to five different types of pearls. They are:

1. **Natural seed pearls**. The term "keshi" was used for these pearls before cultured pearls ever existed.

2. **Pearls that form as by-products of the Japanese Akoya pearl oyster culturing process** from nacre secretion around microorganisms or shell particles that enter the pearl during pearl nucleation. The nacre may also be secreted around detached fragments of mantle tissue inserted with the pearl nuclei. The Akoya oyster has only one grafting and one harvest of cultured pearls and keshi.

3. **Pearls that form as by-products of the South Sea and black pearl oyster culturing process.** These oysters can have up to two re-seedings of nuclei, and thus produce up to three pearls during the oyster's life cycle. Keshi pearls can be found in all three harvests.

4. **Tiny seed-like pearls that form as by-products of the freshwater pearl culturing process** from microorganisms or particles of shell or mud. These are found in the first or second harvest of freshwater pearl mussels.

5. **Chinese reborn freshwater pearls**, which are found in the second harvest. These are keshi-type pearls but not true keshi because they're intentionally cultivated—not formed accidentally. Nevertheless, they're often sold as Chinese freshwater keshi by freshwater pearl dealers.

Because of the confusing use of the term "keshi" and the fact that their origin cannot be proved, labs such as the GIA Gem Trade Lab don't identify keshi on their lab reports. They simply call them cultured pearls or non-beaded cultured pearls.

As of February 2010, CIBJO (the World Jewelry Confederation) defines keshi as a trade term for a non-beaded cultured pearl formed accidentally or intentionally by human intervention in marine (saltwater) pearl oysters such as the Akoya oyster, silver/gold lipped oyster, black-lipped oyster and freshwater mollusks.

Keshi-type pearls also form in American mussels. The American Pearl Company uses the term **lagniappe pearls** to refer to the extra non-beaded pearls that form in American freshwater pearls after they have implanted nuclei in their mussels.

Scallop Pearls: Natural pearls from the scallop "*Nodipecten subnodosus.*" Some people call them "lion's paw pearls" because they come from a scallop whose shell resembles a lion's paw. Until the year 2000, no one in the gem industry had ever seen a natural pearl from this scallop. Scallop pearls, which are found off the coast of California, range in colors from white to deep royal purple with varying shades of oranges, pinks and plums. They are non nacreous with a mosaic pattern that has a flash effect similar to the flame-lake pattern on a conch and melo pearl. These latter two pearls, however, are found in univalve snails instead of in a bivalve scallop. Scallop pearls range in price from $50 to $1000 per carat wholesale.

Mother of Pearl: The smooth, hard pearly lining on the interior of a mollusk shell, which is used to make decorative objects, buttons and beads. Cultured pearls are much more expensive than mother-of-pearl beads even though pearl nacre and mother of pearl are composed of basically the same pearly substance ($CaCO_3$ and a little water and conchiolin, a binding agent). Mother of pearl, however, generally has a slightly higher percentage of water and conchiolin than pearl nacre. Many designs feature mother of pearl. Mother of pearl and oyster shells are also used for carving.

Fig. 3.19 Mother of pearl antique Chinese gaming counter from Timeless Gems. *Photo ©R. Newman.*

Fig. 3.20 Reverse side of gaming counter in figure 3.19 from Timeless Gems. *Photo © R. Newman.*

Fig. 3.22 Lagniappe cultured pearls "In the Clouds and Band" brooch designed by Helen Ringus. *Photo and pearls from the Latendresse Family & American Pearl Company, Inc.*

Fig. 3.21 Keshi-type freshwater pearls from Sea Hunt Pearls. *Photo by Lee-Carraher*

Fig. 3.23 Shell cameo and pearl bracelet. *Cameo jewelry and photo from Rainforest Design®.*

Fig. 3.24 Natural scallop pearls (lion's paw pearls). *Pearls and photo from Pacific Coast Pearls.*

Fig. 3.25 A Mikimoto clasp. *Photo from Mikimoto (America), Ltd.*

Mikimoto Pearls: A brand name for pearls produced and marketed by the Miki-moto Co. Be aware that the Mikimoto name has been misrepresented in some jewelry and discount stores. Therefore, you shouldn't assume that pearls labeled "Mikimoto" are Mikimoto pearls. Look at the clasp. Only those pearls with an 18-karat-gold Mikimoto signature clasp are true Mikimoto pearls. Either a pearl or a diamond will be in the center of it. Also, when you buy Mikimoto pearls, ask the jeweler for the Mikimoto certificate of authenticity that should come with them.

The founder of Mikimoto Pearls, Kokichi Mikimoto, was a pearl farmer, re-searcher and merchant who brought respectability to the cultured pearl. In essence, he is the founder of the cultured pearl industry. He is also credited with inventing most of the techniques of oyster farming used today. In 1907, Tatsuhei Mise and Tokichi Nishikawa in, each became the first to invent techniques for culturing round pearls by using some of Mikimoto's methods.

Mikimoto spent a great deal of time worldwide educating the jewelry trade and the general public about cultured pearls. As a result, cultured pearls became a desir-able commodity and are no longer considered imitations. And Mikimoto, son of a poor noodle vendor, came to be known as "The Pearl King."

Pipi Pearls: Natural pearls from the Cook Islands (also known as Poe Pipi) found in the *Pinctada maculata* oyster, which is probably the smallest pearl producing mollusk. They usually have a white, cream, golden or soft peach color and are named after the Polynesian word *pipi*, meaning "small" or "baby." Typical pearl sizes range from 2mm to 6mm with 8mm being about the maximum size. Golden pipis are the most highly valued.

Pearls Produced by Snails and Clams

Abalone pearls: Even though the abalone is not an oyster or mussel, the colorful nacreous gems it occasionally produces are considered to be pearls. This is because they consist of many concentric layers of nacre. Technically the abalone is classified as a large snail of the genus *Haliotis*.

Abalone pearls are found off the coast of California, Oregon, Alaska, Mexico, Japan, Korea, South Africa, Australia, and New Zealand. (New Zealand abalone mabe pearls are sometimes just called Paua mabe pearls because they are from the Paua abalone). Abalone pearls usually have unique baroque shapes which are sought after by designers, and their colors may be any combination or shade of green, blue, pink, purple, silver, or on rare occasions cream white. Blue and pink colors are especially popular. Fine-quality abalone pearls have an almost metallic-like luster and may vary in price from $200 to $2000 and higher per carat depending on size and quality. Their size can range from seed size to 685 carats, the world's largest abalone pearl. It's in the personal collection of K.C.Bell and is listed in the Guinness Book of Records.

No matter what their size, abalone pearls are rare. Wes Rankin, a dealer who specializes in abalone pearls, estimates that the odds of finding a natural pearl of any size or shape in an abalone is one in 50,000.

Abalone blister pearls are being successfully cultivated, but there have been problems culturing whole abalone pearls. Abalone blood does not coagulate, so when a whole pearl nucleus is surgically implanted into the body of the abalone, it tends to bleed to death.

Fig. 3.26 Natural abalone pearl (156.45 carats) bracelet designed and handmade by Jean Jung. *Photo from Pacific Coast Pearls.*

Fig. 3.27 Gem-quality abalone pearls. The natural pearl jewelry was designed and handmade by Caughie. *Photo from Pacific Coast Pearls.*

Fig. 3.28 Abalone mabe pearls from Blue River Gems and Jewelry. The shell backing is showing on the underside of the drop-shape mabe. *Photo © Renée Newman.*

Fig. 3.29 A polished Korean opal-like blister pearl, a product of abalone perliculture induced by electric acupuncture. *Photo by Matthew Arden.*

Fig. 3.30 Pipi pearls (Poe pipi) from the Kojima Company. *Photo by Sarah Canizzaro.*

Fig. 3.31 Top: Korean cultured whole and mabe abalone pearls. Bottom: a strange pearl formation and a striated mabe produced in a Korean abalone. *Photo by Matthew Arden.*

No surgical cutting is required to produce cultured blister pearls. A nucleus (usually a half-spherical plastic bead) is simply cemented to the inside of the abalone shell, which the abalone later covers with nacre. After a blister pearl is harvested, the nucleus is removed, the hollow area is filled with an artificial substance, and a hard backing is placed over it. It is then sold as a cultured abalone mabe pearl.

Conch Pearls Also called "pink pearls"— though many are orange, brown, white, yellow, or purplish—they are found in the great Conch (pronounced "konk", a large marine snail (Strombus gigas) found throughout the Caribbean. Gemologists consider these "pearls" to be technically a calcareous concretion because their formation is not concentric layers of nacre. They have a porcelain-like surface and like traditional gemstones, they are measured in carats. The most valued conch pearls are symmetrical and have a distinct flame-like pattern and a strong pink or peach color.

Because of the rarity of the conch pearl, even small, pale, irregular ones can retail for more than $500 per carat. Better quality conch pearls may sell for more than $2000 per carat and tend to be sought after primarily by Europeans and Arabs. Non-nacreous conch pearls are exceedingly rare, the average being one for every fifty conch caught. Several countries now control fishing quotas or ban the taking of conch outright.

Knowing the microscopic structure of a pearl and its shell helps identify the source of a pearl. Issue #16 of the SSEF Facette (Jan 2009) stated that the close relationship in structure between shell and pearl means that analytical results gained from the shell are also valid for pearls of the same species. The flame structure of non-nacreous pearls such as conch and melo pearls is due to a crosswise array of bundles of aragonite fibers. Light striking on the side of the bundles is reflected, whereas light falling on the profile of the bundles is absorbed. See figures 3.34 and 3.36..

In November 2009, GIA's G & G E-brief and *Science Daily* (Nov. 5, 2009) announced that attempts to culture conch pearls had finally been successful. Scientists from Florida's Atlantic University's Harbor Branch Oceanographic Institute had developed novel seeding techniques which had enabled them to produce more than 200 beaded and non-beaded cultured pearls from the queen conch. Fortunately, the culturing technique does not require sacrificing the conch in the process. According to *Science Daily*, "The 100 percent survival rate of a queen conch after seeding and the fact that it will produce another pearl after the first pearl is harvested will make this culturing process more efficient and environmentally sustainable for commercial application." X-radiography clearly shows the beads or tissue-related cavities in the beaded and non-beaded samples. The GIA is working with the co-inventors, Drs. Héctor Acosta-Salmón and Megan Davis, to develop other identification criteria to separate cultured conch pearls from their natural counterparts.

Melo Pearls: Form inside sea snails called bailer shells, melon shells or boat shells (*melo melo)*, which are found in the South China Sea off the coast of Vietnam, Malaysia and Singapore. They're non-nacreous, rare and available only as natural pearls. Melo "pearls" are usually oval or round and come in orange, yellow, reddish or brownish colors with a wavy "flame" pattern. They're typically very large, weighing up to more than 200 carats. Large strong orange to orange-red melo pearls can cost thousands of dollars.

Fig. 3.32 New Zealand Paua mabe pearls. *Earrings design © Eve Alfillé; photo: Matt Arden.*

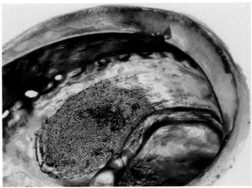

Fig. 3.33 New Zealand abalone (paua) shell from Moana Natural Pearl Co. *Photo by Rob Wright.*

Fig. 3.34 Flame structure as seen on a pink conch pearl with brighter and darker areas. *H. A. Hänni © SSEF Swiss Gemmological Institute.*

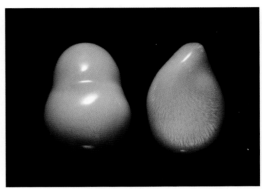

Fig. 3.35 Conch pearls with flame pattern from Pala International. *Photo by Mia Dixon.*

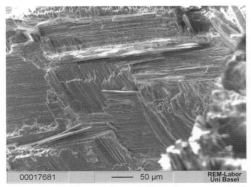

Fig. 3.36 Broken surface of *Strombus gigas* shell (pink conch) showing a criss cross orientation. The laths consist of aragonite and form in layers. *Photo Marcel Düggelin, ZMB. Courtesy H. A. Hänni © SSEF Swiss Gemmological Institute.*

Fig. 3.37 Conch pearl and diamond bracelet created by Busatti. *Photo from Luca Busatti.*

Fig. 3.38 Conch shell. *Photo and shell from Mikimoto (America) Ltd.*

Fig. 3.39 Conch pearl strand from Kojima Company. *Photo by Sarah Canizzaro.*

Fig. 3.40 Melo pearl 37.88 ct.s from Pala International with distinct flame pattern. *Photo: Mia Dixon.*

Fig. 3.41 Melo pearl (75.07 cts) from Pala International with flame pattern. *Photo by Mia Dixon.*

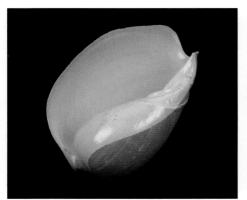

Fig. 3.42 Melo pearl baler shell from Pala International. *Photo by Mia Dixon.*

Fig. 3.43 Another view of a baler shell from Pala International. *Photo by Mia Dixon.*

Fig. 3.44 Quahog pearls from Kojima Company. *Photo by Sarah Canizzaro.*

Fig. 3.45 World's largest abalone pearl—685 carats. *Photo & pearl from K. C. Bell.*

Fig. 3.47 *Nautilus pompilius* blister pearl. *Photo and pearl from Stephen Metzler.*

Fig. 3.46 Five-pound giant clam pearl held by journalist-gemologist Diana Jarrett. *Pearl from Bonhams & Butterfields; photo courtesy Diana.*

Fig. 3.48 Diamond-studded, carved black pearl pendant by Chi Galatea Huynh. *Photo from Galatea.*

Fig. 3.49 Faceted Tahitian cultured pearl. *Ring by Mark Schneider Design; photo: Daniel Van Rossen.*

Quahog Pearls: Clam pearls from the bivalve clam *Venus mercenaria* (also called the *Mercenaria mercenaria*). This common hard clam is found along the North Atlantic coast of the United States and has a purple stain on the back of the shell. Quahog (pronounced KOH-hog) pearls occur in various colors. White is the least rare and often the most economical color, while purple to lavender colors are the rarest and most valuable. Other colors include beige, brown and black. Usually the more uniform the color, the higher the price, with the exception of some pearls with attractive bicolor and tricolor patterns. Most quahog pearls are below seven millimeters but exceptionally large pearls can range from 14 to 20 millimeters.

Giant Clam Pearls. Rare pearls from the *Tridacna gigas, Tridacna squamosa,* or *Hippopus hippopus*, which can reach a size of several centimeters and are white or occasionally light pink or yellowish. Some have a flame pattern. The best known giant clam pearls are those from the *Tridacna gigas*. An example is the "Palawan Princess" pearl shown in figure 3.46. It was found off the Philippine Coast, measures six inches in diameter and is valued at between $300,000 and $400.000. The pearl is thought to be surpassed in size only by the 14-pound "Pearl of Allah," a 31,893.5-carat Tridacna gigas pearl that was also found off the coastal waters of the Philippines.

Nautilus Pearl: A very rare pearl from the *Nautilus pompilius,* a cephalopod, which is a class of mollusks that includes squids and octopuses. The *Nautilus* pearl usually has a non-lustrous white color and a baroque or pearl shape and is found mainly in Southeast Asia and the southwestern Pacific Ocean.

Pearl scholar Blaire Beavers says, "There has been controversy over the existence of pearls from the *Nautilus pompilius,* because the inside of the shell is nacreous, but the pearls are not. Pearls have been submitted for testing, but no discernible chemical or spectral difference exists between a Nautilus pearl and a *Tridacna* pearl. The smaller *Tridacna squamosa* clam pearl looks very similar, but it appears that some nautilus pearls have a 'polar swirl. (See close-up photo by Steve Metzler, fig. 3.47.) In order to settle it once and for all, interested parties launched a quest to find an attached blister pearl on a nautilus shell, preferably out of existing shell stock so a live nautilus would not be killed. This pearl was the first one found.

"The photo is of that very same pearl, technically a button pearl that started out as a free pearl, but caught on the lip of the chamber and was found attached to the shell by a thick thread. If it hadn't attached, it probably would have been expelled. It's 8.8mm across by 7mm high and weighs 4.4 carats. The owner, rare pearl collector Stephen Metzler, is very excited about it."

Faceted Pearls: Pearls used to be just smooth and unpolished, but recently more and more faceted pearls have appeared on the market. The faceting creates a sparkling effect and allows pearl producers to polish away flaws that would otherwise detract from the beauty of the pearl (figs. 3.31, 3.32). Faceted freshwater pearls are available in a wide variety of treated and untreated colors.

Gem-studded Pearls: Another creative way of eliminating pearl flaws is to drill them away and set the drilled areas with diamonds or colored gems. Gem-studded pearls have a distinctive look that's made them popular with jewelry designers.

4

Pearl Shapes

Shape can play a major role in determining the price of pearls. Throughout history, round has generally been considered the most valuable shape for a pearl. Perhaps this was because pearls were considered a symbol of the moon. Nevertheless, the most famous and valuable pearls are often not round. That's because factors such as size, luster, nacre quality and origin are also important.

Akoya pearls can be divided into four basic shape categories (fig. 4.1):

Round So symmetrical that the pearl will roll in a straight line on a flat inclined surface. Normally this is the most expensive shape, provided the pearl has an adequate nacre coating.

Off-Round Slightly flattened or ovoid.

Semi-Baroque Obviously not round. Pear, drop, egg and button shapes are examples.

Baroque Very distorted and irregular in shape. Frequently, the surface is uneven. These pearls occasionally resemble familiar objects such as teeth, mushrooms, cacti, tadpoles, or snails. High-quality pearls of varying degrees of baroqueness can fetch more money than very thin coated round pearls.

Sometimes additional categories are added for evaluating shape. For example, the subcategories of "mostly round" and "slightly off-round" may also be used along with the four basic categories above.

Akoya pearl prices are generally based on round pearls. When the pearls deviate from the round shape, they are discounted. Baroque pearls, for example, may be sold for 55% to 80% less than rounds. Pearl pricing varies from one dealer to another.

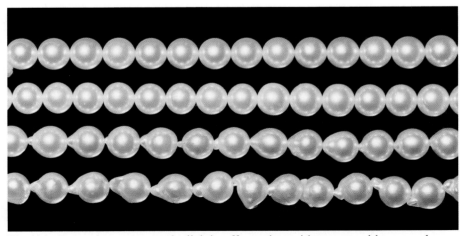

Fig. 4.1 Top to bottom—round, slightly off round, semi-baroque and baroque shapes. *Photo © Renée Newman..*

South Sea White, Golden and Black Pearl Shapes

Perfectly round South Sea pearls are far more rare than Akoya pearls, which are smaller and have thinner nacre. The thicker nacre and longer growth periods of South Sea pearls lead to a wide variety of shapes. These cannot be described adequately with just the four Akoya shape categories of round, off-round, semi-baroque and baroque. Some of the most common terms used to describe South Sea pearl shape are as follows:

Round: So symmetrical that the pearl will roll in a straight line on a flat inclined surface. Normally this is the most expensive shape.

Semi-round or **off-round:** Almost round, but the pearl will wobble or deviate to one side as you roll it.

Oval: An elongated round shape. It sells for much less than rounds.

Drop: Rounded at one end and elongated or pointed at the opposite end. The extension or tail corresponds to the incision where the nucleus was inserted.

There are several variations of the drop shape. A few are shown in figure 4.3. The drop shape is sometimes described as **semi-baroque**, especially if it's asymmetrical. The more symmetrical a drop shape is, the greater its value. Very symmetrical drops with a smooth top and pleasing shape are called "perfect drops" or "knock-out drops" by some dealers.

Pear: A drop shape with a slightly concave waist. Some people use the terms "drop" and "pear" interchangeably.

Button: Rounded on one side and flatter on the other. The width is greater than the height. Buttons generally sell for less than drops and rounded shapes except in sizes over 16 mm where they are used for earrings. A round pearl of 17 mm sticks out too far from the ear, while a button makes an ideal earring. Since there's a high demand for buttons over 16 mm, their prices are high.

Acorn: Resembles an acorn. Has a high dome shape and flat bottom. This shape is practical for earring drops and brooches, but there is less demand for it than for the button shape.

Triangle: Has a pointed or drop-shaped top and a flat bottom. Short triangles may be used for stud-type earrings, and long triangles can be used for pendants and dangling earrings.

Circle or **circled:** Has one or more parallel, ring-like furrows or grooves around the entire circumference of the pearl. These circular formations do not occur as often in white and yellow South Sea pearls as in those which are dark-colored. Circled shapes sell for much less than the previous shapes. Circles or rims can be present on drops, ovals, off-rounds, triangles and buttons.

Baroque: Irregular or freeform. This shape is often preferred by designers because it's unique. Generally, the baroque and circled pearls are the lowest priced shapes.

No matter what their shape, South Sea pearls are generally sold undrilled if they are not on a strand. This allows the buyer to determine how the pearls will be used or mounted. Be willing to compromise on shape. This may be necessary due to the high price and limited availability of round South Sea pearls.

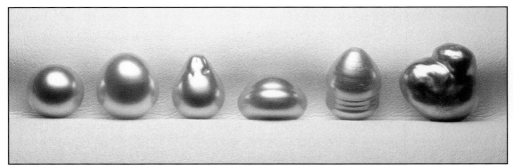

Fig. 4.2 Some South Sea pearl shapes, right to left: round, oval, drop, button, circle, baroque. These general categories don't always give a clear visual image of shape. A better description of the circled pearl shape might be circled bullet or circled drop. *Pearls from King Plutarco, Inc. Photo © Renée Newman.*

Fig. 4.3 Drops come in a wide range of shapes and sizes. The drops with the smoothest tops and most symmetrical form are usually priced the highest, all other factors being equal; but designers often prefer unique, asymmetrical shapes. *Pearls from King Plutarco, Inc. Photo © Renée Newman.*

Fig. 4.3 An interesting assortment of pearl shapes. Finding matches for pearls with distinctive shapes and colors is challenging. *Pearls from Eliko Pearl. Photo © Renée Newman.*

When you need to cut down on the price, shape is a good category to compromise on. In fact, baroque and circled pearls often make more interesting jewelry pieces than round pearls do.

Judging Pearl Shape

When judging pearls for shape, take into consideration the type of pearl you are looking at. For example, expensive natural pearls are typically baroque, whereas cheap cultured pearls with thin nacre (pearl coating) are generally round. That's because natural pearls don't contain a round nucleus bead, and cultured pearl beads that are hardly coated with nacre don't have much of a chance to grow into irregular shapes. The typical shapes of five pearl types are described below to help you learn what degree of roundness to expect of pearls. They are listed from the most commonly round to the most commonly baroque.

Akoya pearls with thin nacre	Often round
Akoya pearls with thick nacre	Frequently off-round, but round ones are available too. Baroque Akoya pearl strands are considered low quality.
South Sea cultured	Rarely perfectly round. The larger the pearl, the more it will tend to deviate from round. Baroques are often regarded as a good alternative to the more expensive symmetrical shapes when one's budget is limited.
Natural saltwater	Usually baroque or semi-baroque. Round ones are extremely rare.
Freshwater, cultured & natural	Frequently baroque, especially if they are natural. Baroque freshwater pearls are considered desirable. Cultured off-round freshwater pearls are also readily available. They are normally much more affordable than saltwater pearls of similar quality and size.

Another grading factor to consider when judging off-round and especially semi-baroque pearls is their **degree of symmetry** (perfectly round pearls are always symmetrical and baroque pearls are by definition asymmetrical). If for example, you are buying a teardrop pearl pendant for someone special, one with two equal sides would probably be the most desirable. Lopsided pearls can be interesting, but they are considered less valuable than those which are symmetrical.

Even though dealers agree round is the most expensive shape, there is no standardized system for determining how shape affects pearl prices. The way pearls are discounted for shape variation can differ from one dealer to another. Don't let this lack of standardization lead you to ignore pearl shape as a value factor. Consider it important, and keep in mind when judging pearl prices that it's best to compare pearls of the same shape as well as the same size, color, type and luster.

5

Judging Luster & Nacre Thickness

"PEARLS—HALF OFF!"

Does this indicate a bargain? Who knows? It might even mean "Nacre—Half Off." No matter what their price, pearls aren't much of a bargain if they're dull-looking or their nacre (pearl coating, pronounced NAY-ker) peels away.

Normally thin nacre means low luster, but there are thin-nacre pearls with good luster and thick-nacre pearls with low luster. Consequently, it's best to treat luster and nacre thickness as two separate value factors.

What is Pearl Luster?

The noted gemologist, Robert Webster, defines **luster** as the surface brilliancy of a gemstone, which depends on the quality and quantity of the reflected light. When the term "luster" is applied to pearls, it tends to have a broader meaning. It also refers to the light reflected off the internal layers of nacre. In other words, a lustrous pearl has more than just a shiny, reflective surface. It also has a glow from within.

For example, compare the pearl to a highly polished gold bead. The gold bead will usually have sharper surface reflections than the pearl, but that doesn't mean it's more lustrous. In fact, it's more conventional to describe gold as shiny, bright or metallic. Brilliant pearls, on the other hand, are more frequently termed lustrous.

Pearls with a very high luster will generally show the following characteristics when viewed under a bare light with the naked eye:

- Strong light reflections
- Sharp light reflections
- A good contrast between the bright and darker areas of the pearl

Many pearl experts would also list iridescence as a characteristic because lustrous pearls not only reflect light, they break it up into different colors. On round pearls the iridescence tends to be very subtle, and a pinkish tone may result. On high luster baroque pearls, you may see flashes of rainbow colors. Since iridescence is a color phenomenon, this book has it listed as a quality factor in the chapter on color.

What Determines Luster?

The luster of a pearl depends on the quality of the nacre—its transparency, smoothness and overall thickness as well as the thickness of each of the microscopic layers of nacre. Under an electron microscope, the nacre crystals of lustrous pearls have a strong hexagonal form and are regularly distributed, whereas the crystals forming the nacre of lifeless pearls lack a clear outline, are thinly scattered or are irregularly deposited (from *The Retail Jeweller's Guide*, p 90, by Kenneth Blakemore).

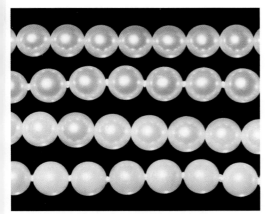 

Fig. 5.1 Top to bottom: High luster, medium luster, low luster and very low luster. Note how the dark areas become lighter as the luster decreases.

Fig. 5.2 Same pearls viewed against a white background. *Photos 5.1 and 5.2 © Renée Newman.*

The quality of the nacre, and in turn the luster, is affected by a variety of factors such as:

- Cultivation techniques used
- Cultivation place
- Health of mother oyster
- Length of time pearl is in oyster
- Time of year when pearl is harvested
- Unusually wide variations in temperature
- Pollution
- Natural disasters such as earthquakes and typhoons
- Type of oyster used. For example, the mabe oyster *Pteria penguin* (found mainly in the tropical seas of Southeast Asia) can produce a pearl with a higher luster than those of the South Seas silver-lip oyster. The Akoya oyster is also noted for its capacity to produce pearls of high luster.

High luster is not merely the result of leaving a pearl in an Akoya oyster for an adequate length of time. In fact, cultivating a lustrous pearl is a complex process, involving both skill and chance.

Judging Luster

Suppose we could line up all the pearls in the world according to the quality of their luster. We would notice that a very low percentage of the pearls would be at the end of the line with the best luster. We would also notice that the pearls would very gradually change in luster as we went down the line. In other words, there would be no distinct luster categories.

We could, however, divide the line of pearls into any number of equal ranges (categories) of luster. Then we could assign a luster name to each category such as **very high**, **high**, **medium**, **low and very low**. Luster categories like this are used by many gemologists and appraisers. Pearl dealers have their own in-house grading systems, which often combine various value factors. However, not all dealers agree about what each grade represents. For example, some dealers think the terms **"gem quality"** or **"AAAA"** should only be applied to pearls having an exceptionally high luster, while others use the terms for a broader range of luster. As a result, you shouldn't assume, that a pearl strand labeled "AAAA" or "Gem" is necessarily top quality. In fact, it's a common practice to misuse grades by applying high ones to lower quality goods.

Very high luster pearls have sharp, intense, almost mirror-like light reflections, and there is a high contrast between their bright and dark areas. Such pearls are not always easy to find. In fact, you may be lucky to find a store in your area that has them in stock. Expect to pay premium prices for these pearls. The actual cost of the strands will be determined by a variety of factors.

Very low luster pearls are easy to spot. They look very milky or chalky, and seem more like a white bead than a pearl. This is a result of the low contrast between the light and dark areas of the pearls. Some jewelers won't stock this type of pearl, but others will. This is also the type of pearl a mail order outfit might be tempted to sell. That's because the customer doesn't see what he's getting—he only sees the super low price listed in the catalogue.

The majority of the pearls sold in stores probably fall in the low and medium luster ranges. Many fine-quality jewelry stores also stock high-luster pearls. The best way to learn to recognize high-, medium-, and low-luster pearls is to look at strands representing these luster ranges. Some jewelers may show you short master strands illustrating these or similar categories, but they may use different category names such as "bright," "commercial," "AAA," etc. Top-quality pearl salespeople are eager to help you see luster differences so you'll know what you are getting for your money. They don't want their prices unfairly compared to stores offering low-quality "bargain" pearls.

As of 2010, the GIA Pearl description system lists five categories of luster:

Excellent—Reflections are bright, sharp, and distinct

Very good—Reflections appear bright and near sharp

Good—Reflections are bright but not sharp; they're slightly hazy around the edges

Fair—Reflections are weak, hazy, and blurred

Poor—Reflections are dim and diffused

As you shop for pearls and examine them for luster, keep in mind that the pearl industry has not yet adopted a standardized system for grading pearls. What one jeweler considers low or fair luster another might call medium or good luster. Therefore, **don't rely just on word descriptions of pearls.** What your eyes see is what counts most. Verbal descriptions are merely guides. If you have any strands of pearls at home, it's a good idea to take them along and use them as a basis for comparison. Even pearl dealers rely on comparison strands when buying pearls.

Also keep in mind the following tips when shopping:

● Examine the strands on a flat white surface, e.g., a white cloth, board or paper. Luster can be hard to judge when pearls are on a dark surface or suspended.

● Look at the light reflections on the pearls. Usually, the less sharp and intense they are, the lower the luster. Sometimes, however, a lack of sharpness is due to surface blemishes, rather than the overall luster.

● If possible, examine the pearls directly under a light instead of away from the light. This helps bring out their luster. (Lighting is discussed more in detail in the next section).

- Look for the brightest and darkest areas of the pearls. Then compare the contrast between the two. The lower the contrast and the milkier the pearl, the lower the luster. This is one of the quickest and easiest ways to spot low and very low luster. Milky-looking pearls are sometimes sold in "high quality" stores. Be aware that their luster is low.

- Compare the lusters of the individual pearls on the strand. They will almost always vary somewhat in luster. The luster quality of a strand is determined by its overall appearance, not just by one pearl. High-luster strands, however, should not have low- and very-low-luster pearls.

- Roll the pearls slightly so you can see their entire surface. The luster not only varies from pearl to pearl; it varies on each individual pearl.

- Try the pearls on and check if you can see the highlighted spots on them from a distance (say 10 feet/3 meters). You'll be able to if the pearls are of good quality.

- If possible, lay the pearls alongside other strands and compare the lusters. This is most effective when you already know the relative quality of the comparison strands. Keep in mind that your impression of a strand will be affected by the pearls it is compared to. A strand will look better when viewed next to lower-luster strands than next to those of higher luster.

Sometimes buyers get so involved in examining the shape and blemishes of pearls that they overlook their luster. The Japan Pearl Exporters' Association would consider this a big mistake. According to their booklet *Cultured Pearls*, "The most important value point in pearls of equal size is luster because that is what gives a pearl its beauty."

How Lighting Affects Luster

Gemologists and appraisers normally grade pearls under standardized lighting conditions. When shopping for pearls, you will encounter various lighting situations. You need to understand, therefore, how lighting affects the appearance of pearls in order to avoid being misled.

The main thing to remember is the stronger and more direct the light, the more lustrous the pearls will look. Ask yourself:

- Is the lighting diffused? For example, is the light covered with a white shade? Is the light coming through curtains, clouds or translucent glass? Is it a fluorescent light instead of a bare bulb? The more diffused the light is, the lower the luster will appear to be. Bare lights or direct sunlight, on the other hand, will bring out the luster of pearls (figs. 5.2 to 5.4).

- How intense is the light? In the case of sunlight, is it early morning or midday? Midday sunlight will bring out the luster more. In the case of light bulbs, what is their wattage? The higher the wattage, the more lustrous your pearls will look.

- How close is the light to the pearls? The further the light is from the pearls, the smaller and less intense the reflections become and the less the pearls seem to glow (figs. 5.2 & 5.3). If it's possible for you to carry or wear comparison strands of pearls, do so. You'll be able to compare known strands with unknown ones under equal lighting conditions, and it will be easier for you to tell the effect of the lighting on both.

How Lighting Affects Pearl Color and Luster

Fig. 5.3 Mabe pearls ranging from high to low luster viewed under a 100-watt light bulb 4 feet (1.2 meters) away. *Photo © Renée Newman.*

Fig. 5.4 Same pearls under a lamp with a 100-watt light bulb one foot (30 cm) away. The light reflection is stronger, the luster appears higher, and the overtones are more noticeable. *Photo © Renée Newman.*

Fig. 5.5 Same pearls under a lamp with a 100-watt bulb diffused with paper and viewed 1 foot (30 cm) away. The diffusion reduces luster and the strength of the overtone colors. *Photo © Renée Newman.*

Judging Nacre Thickness

If you were to cut a 7-mm Akoya cultured pearl in half, you would see a large core inside. It would be a bead probably cut from an American mussel shell. The outside of the bead would be encircled with a pearly layer of nacre. If the pearl had been left in the oyster for just six months, the layer would be very thin, too thin to be very durable or lustrous.

Before about 1960, Japanese Akoya pearl farmers left the pearls in the oyster for at least2 ½ years. Mikimoto left his in for more than three years for maximum nacre thickness. Then many farmers dropped the time to one and a half years. Around 1979, pearl harvesting started to be done just after six to eight months. The result—many inexpensive, low-quality pearls on the market. And they are still out there, being offered at rock-bottom prices. The buyers end up with shell beads and hardly any pearl. Fortunately, better pearls with thicker nacre are also available, but rarely as thick as those cultured before the 1960's. The goal of this section is to help you determine if the nacre thickness of the pearls you look at is acceptable or not.

The GIA (Gemological Institute of America) defined five levels of nacre thickness for Akoya cultured pearls in their pearl grading course that was copyrighted in 1990:

Very thick   At least 0.5 mm on all the pearls of the strand

Thick   At least 0.5 mm on most pearls of the strand

Medium   0.35–0.5 mm on most pearls

Thin   0.25–0.35 mm on most pearls

Very thin   0.25 mm or less on most pearls

The GIA's 2001 categorization of nacre quality has three classifications.

Acceptable—Nucleus not noticeable, no chalky appearance

Nucleus visible—The cultured pearl shows evidence of its bead nucleus through the nacre

Chalky appearance—The cultured pearl has a dull appearance

GIA lab reports express nacre thickness as an average measurement in millimeters.

Pearl dealers don't need to measure the nacre to determine if it's thin or very thin. They know just by looking at the pearls. Some clues are:

- The pearls usually have a low or very low luster and may look milky. Some thin-coated pearls, however, may show a decent medium luster.
- The nacre coating has cracks.
- Areas are visible where the nacre has peeled off (figs. 5.6 & 5.7)
- Layers of the shell beads are slightly visible when the pearls are suspended and light shines through them. These layers look like curved lines, stripes or wood grain. Usually the thinner the nacre, the easier it is to see the lines. Figure 5.8 is an example of what the shell layers look like in a thinly-coated pearl with light shining through it. If you can't see any shell layers, this does not mean that the nacre is thick. There are lots of thinly-coated pearls that don't show these layers. However, if you can see them, the nacre is probably too thin.

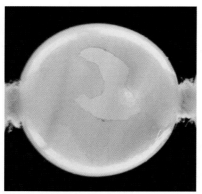

Fig. 5.6 Pearl with nacre so thin it is peeling off. *Photo © Renée Newman.*

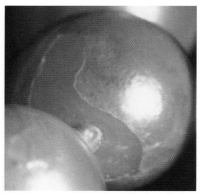

Fig. 5.7 Pearl with very thin nacre peeling near drill hole. *Photo © R. Newman.*

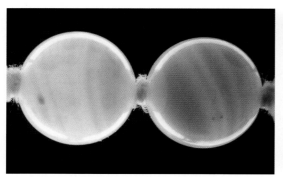

Fig. 5.8 Light and dark views of pearls with thin nacre. Note the curved stripes which indicate the growth layers of the shell bead nucleus. *Photo © Renée Newman.*

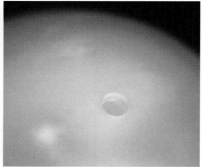

Fig. 5.9 Drill-hole showing acceptable nacre thickness. *Photo © Renée Newman.*

● As the beads are rolled, some may look light and then dark as the light shines through them. This is because the shell beads may have mother-of-pearl layers that block the light. This phenomenon is called "blinking" and can sometimes be seen in thinly coated pearls. Figure 5.8 is an example of two pearls with very thin nacre in the light position and dark position. When rotated, each of these pearls "blinks." Pearls with thick nacre should not blink.

A more accurate way of judging nacre thickness is by examining the drill holes of the pearls (figs 5.7 & 5.9), preferably with a 10-power magnifier such as a jeweler's hand loupe.

Examining drill holes with a loupe will also help you detect dyes and imitations. The drill-hole method is too slow to be practical for dealers, but it's a good way for less-skilled people to estimate nacre thickness. It also allows appraisers to give a more objective measure of nacre thickness.

If you have some pearls at home, try examining their drill holes with a loupe under a good light. Find the dividing line between the nacre and the bead. Then look at a millimeter ruler with the loupe to get a visual image of a 0.35-mm thickness.

Compare this thickness to that of the nacre. Seeing actual examples of thin, medium and thick nacre is an easier way to learn to tell the difference.

This book suggests 0.35 mm as a minimum nacre thickness because it has been mentioned in the trade as a minimum. For example, Hiroshi Komatsu of the Tokyo Mikimoto research lab is quoted as saying, "Our tests show the best luster and color occur with at least 0.35 mm of nacre, and Mikimoto pearls are always thicker" (as quoted by Fred Ward in the August 1985 issue of *National Geographic*). The nacre thickness may not be the same throughout a pearl. Nacre measurements can also vary depending on the measuring instrument used and the person doing the measuring. So consider the 0.35-mm minimum as an approximate thickness.

When you have your pearls appraised, ask if nacre thickness is indicated on the report. Also ask how the appraiser's nacre-thickness categories are defined in terms of millimeter thickness. A term such as "thin" can vary from one person to another, so definitions are necessary. There must be a drill hole or other opening on a pearl for an accurate estimate of nacre thickness to be made visually.

Also make sure that the millimeter thickness is of the radius of the pearl, not of the diameter, which would be twice the nacre thickness along the radius. If someone tells you the average nacre thickness of an Akoya pearl is 1 mm, figure they have doubled it. Today it's hard to find Akoya pearls with even a 0.4-mm thickness.

It's not deceptive to sell thin-nacre pearls as long as the thin nacre and its consequences are disclosed to buyers. Ideally, consumers could choose from a wide range of nacre thicknesses and know exactly what they were getting for their money. Since this ideal does not currently exist, it's to your advantage to pay attention to nacre thickness and to learn to detect thin nacre yourself.

Is Nacre Thickness Important and Does it Affect Pricing?

As you shop, you may encounter pearl salespeople who claim nacre thickness is unimportant and has no effect upon price. Beware. All their pearls may be of low quality. Ask them, "Why is something which affects the beauty and durability of my pearls unimportant?"

As for price, it has to be affected by nacre thickness. It naturally will cost a farmer progressively more to culture pearls for six months, one year and 1 1/2 years. The additional cost must be passed on to the buyers.

Often the effect of nacre thickness on price is linked to that of luster. Thicker nacre usually means higher luster, and both bring higher prices.

The Mikimoto Company thinks nacre thickness is important. One of their advisors, Shigeru Miki, made the following statement in the August 1985 *National Geographic* article by Fred Ward: "The most important quality of a cultured pearl is thickness of the nacre. It gives color, luster, and appearance. Pearls are among the softest of all gems, and normal body fluids, as well as contact with perfumes, hair sprays, and acids reduce nacre. A thinly coated pearl won't last many years."

Golay Buchel, a company with branches in Europe, North America and the Orient, discusses luster and nacre thickness in its booklet *Pearls*. They are listed as separate value factors and both are described as important. Golay Buchel's advice to consumers (p. 34): "Remain flexible with regards to colour, size, shape and light surface markings, but **never** make concessions regarding the thickness of the coating."

Judging Color

If you were buying Swiss cheese and you had a choice between a stark white or creamy yellow variety, which would you choose? Most likely you'd pick the cream color variety because the average person has been conditioned to expect Swiss cheese to have a creamy or yellowish tint. If when you bought Swiss cheese, you discovered that pieces with large holes often tasted better than those without, you might also develop a preference for Swiss cheese with big holes.

People's expectation of what pearls should look like have been conditioned in a similar manner. Many expect pearls to be white because that is what they are accustomed to seeing. However, that perception is changing because of the wide variety of colors of freshwater and South Sea pearls that have appeared on the market in recent years.

There are many factors to consider when choosing the color of pearls. The topic of color will also be addressed in the chapters on freshwater, black and South Sea pearls.

Pearl Color

Pearl color is complex. It's a combination of:

Body Color: The predominant basic color of the pearl.

Overtone: The one or more colors that overlie the body color. On black pearls these colors are usually eas-est to see in the lighter areas of the pearl.

Fig. 6.1 A variety of natural-color South Seas and freshwater pearls (10-12 mm) from King's Ransom. *Photo by Betty Sue King.*

On white pearls they are easier to see in the darker areas. For example, lay some white pearls on something white, and look at them under a strong, direct light. (Midday sun is ideal but a light bulb will do.) The outer rim area of the pearls, which is reflecting the white background, will be lighter than the center of the pearls if they are of decent quality (except for the bright reflection of the light). If you look closely, you should see a slight pink, green, blue and/or silver color in the central dark areas of the pearls. This is the overtone. Generally you will see more than one overtone color in a strand of pearls (fig. 6.4). You may also see more than one overtone color on the same pearl.

Fig. 6.2 Pearls with various body and overtone colors viewed under a bare lightbulb. *Pearls from King Plutarco; photo © Renée Newman.*

Fig. 6.3 Natural-color Tahitian pearls with various body colors. *Necklace from Sea Hunt Pearls; photo by Lee-Carraher.*

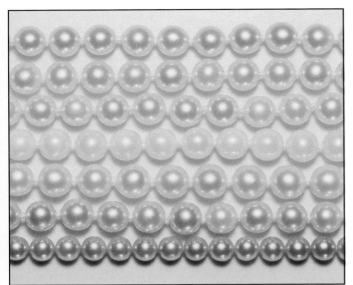

light pink—pink overtones

white—pink & green overtones

white—green & silver overtones

low quality white

cream—mostly pink overtones

yellow—various overtones

dyed yellow (golden)

Fig. 6.4 Akoya pearls come in a range of colors. Specifying pearl color, however, is not easy. Body color, overtones and iridescence must all be considered. To complicate matters, the pearls within a strand vary in color. *Pearls from Shima Pearl; photo © R. Newman.*

Fig. 6.5 Green and pink overtones on a South Sea pearl from Ernie & Regina Goldberger.

Fig. 6.7 Freshwater pearl with high natural iridescencefrom Kojima Co. *Photo by Sarah Canizzaro.*

Fig. 6.6 An example of pink and green overtones on a Tahitian black pearl button clasp. These overtones are frequently found together on high-quality black pearls. The absence of overtones is a sign of low quality. *Pearls & photo from Assael International.*

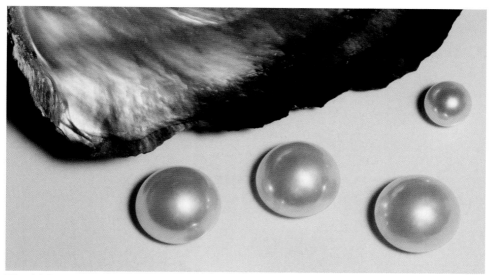

Fig. 6.8 Top quality mabe and Akoya light pink pearls with blue and pink overtones. As you move the pearls, they appear to change color due to their pearly iridescence. The overtone colors are most apparent when the pearls are viewed against a white background under a strong direct light such as a light-bulb. *Pearls from Jye's International; photo © Renée Newman.*

Iridescence: A play of lustrous colors. They may be like those of the rainbow, or they may be a subtle combination of colors such as pink, blue, green and silver as seen in the pearls of figures 6.7 and 6.8. The colors of the pearls change when you move them in your hand.

Orient is another term that is used to refer to pearl iridescence. Some dealers, however, employ the term more loosely to also mean a combination of overtone colors. The 2010 GIA pearl course defines "orient" as "multiple overlying colors or surface iridescence." Other dealers and many books written in the past use the term "orient" to refer to luster because iridescence and luster are interconnected. Since "orient" may be interpreted in various ways, this book primarily uses the term "iridescence" instead.

When you shop for pearls, you may come across terms such as **white rosé**. This means white pearls with a pink overtone. "Rosé" is the French word for pink.

Pink rosé means that most of the pearls have a light pink body color and a pink overtone. White pearls with a silver overtone may be described as **silver(y) white**. Often salespeople don't specify the overtone but they'll simply use one color such as "pink" to describe their overall impression of the pearls. Most pink Akoya pearls have been "pinked" with dye, so there is not a price premium for them.

Judging Pearl Color

When deciding what color pearls to buy, your primary concern should be what looks best on you. But you will also want to know how the color affects their price.

Fig. 6.9 Top grade natural-color (no bleach or dye) white Akoya pearls (7.5–8 mm) with pink and blue overtones. *Hanadama pearls and photo from Jeremy Shepherd at Pearl Paradise.*

The overall body color can play a significant role in determining the price of pearls. The main **body color categories** for Akoya pearls are:

Light pink or white: These are the highest priced Akoya colors. Some dealers used to charge more for light pink pearls, but now, white pearls with high luster sell for about the same as those that are light pink. Most pinkish Akoya pearls on the market have been tinted, particularly those with a strong pink color, and as a result, do not merit a higher price than white pearls. An example of top-grade Akoya pearls that haven't been bleached or pinked is shown in figure 6.9.

Light Cream: Usually this color costs less than white. The higher the quality of the pearls, the greater the price difference will probably be between light cream and white. In low qualities, there may be no difference.

Cream: These usually cost less than light cream. In cream colors, the general tendency is the darker the color, the lower the price. Cream-color pearls are sometimes termed **champagne pearls**.

Dark Cream & Yellow: These colors may be priced about 40% or more lower than white Akoya pearls. The darker the cream or yellow color, the greater the price difference.

When judging color, keep in mind that there is no standardized system of communicating or grading color in the pearl industry. What one dealer calls light cream, another might call cream. Nevertheless, there is an awareness of the concept "cream color" and general agreement that cream-color Akoya pearls tend to cost less than those which are pink or white.

Overtone color(s) may or may not affect the price. The three most common overtones are pink, green and silver. If the color of the overtones has an effect on price, it will generally be as follows:

Pink overtones	Can increase the price
Silver overtones	Usually no effect
Green overtones	Sometimes may decrease the price slightly

The combination of blue and pink overtones is associated with top-quality pearls. Some Japanese dealers describe the color of the most valued Akoya pearls as a bluish-pink, which in essence is a light-pink or white body color with blue and pink overtones. These pearls, which are extremely rare and difficult to find in America, are some-times classified by the Japanese as "hanadama quality " when they have a very high luster and thick nacre.

There is no general agreement in the trade as to how overtones affect price. Most dealers, however, would probably concede that Akoya pearls with pink overtones tend to be more highly valued than those with green ones. This explains why pearls are often dyed pink but not green. What counts most about overtone is how it affects your overall impression of the color and luster of the pearls. Pearl dealers would agree, too, that the presence of overtones is highly desirable. Their absence is a sign of low luster and thin nacre.

The third color component of pearls, **iridescence**, is rarely obvious on round Akoya pearls. It tends to be very subtle combination of pink, blue and green. A more obvious iridescence—flashes of rainbow colors—is more likely to be seen on freshwater pearls and baroque shapes. Iridescence is always considered a positive value factor.

When examining pearls for color remember the following tips:

- Judge the color of pearls against a non-reflective white background. Pearls not only reflect the color of the background, they also *absorb* it. Afterwards, place the pearls on your hand or around your neck to see how they look on you.

- Take into consideration the lighting (see next section). If possible look at the pearls under different types of light sources—daylight near a window, fluorescent, and incandescent (light bulbs). You'll probably be wearing the pearls under a variety of light sources.

- It's a lot easier to compare color than to remember it. If possible, wear or take along some comparison pearls. Otherwise, compare the color to other pearls in the store. Even using white and cream-colored papers as color references is better than relying on color memory.

- When pearl strands are exactly adjacent, their color may seem to bleed from one strand to another. Therefore, also compare them slightly separated from each other.

- Every now and then, look away from the pearls at other colors and objects. When you focus on one color too long, your perception of it becomes distorted.

- Consider how evenly distributed the color is on the pearl(s), especially if it's one major pearl on a ring or pendant. A uniform color is more highly valued than a blotchy one.

- If you are trying to decide between white and pink pearls of the same quality but the pink pearls cost more, look in a few of the drill holes with a 10-power magnifier. If you can see red or pink stains on the nacre layer or a pink line between the nacre and the nucleus, they are dyed (see Chapter 14 about treatments). Seeing positive indications of dye may influence your decision. By the way, even if you don't see evidence of dye, the pearls may still be dyed.

- Make sure you're alert and feel good when you examine pearls. If you're tired, sick or under the influence of alcohol or drugs, your perception of color will be impaired.

Pearls: the Wedding Jewel

The tradition of giving pearls to brides probably dates back to about 1000 BC when the Hindu God Krishna gave his daughter pearls on her wedding day. It continued with the ancient Greeks, who believed that pearls would ensure a happy marriage. The association between pearls and weddings reached a peak during the 14th and 15th centuries when everyone from the bride to her male guests were adorned with pearls.

Today pearls, which symbolize purity and innocence, are as much a wedding jewel as diamonds. Just have a look at a bridal shop or wedding catalogue. You'll find pearls, both imitation and real, decorating wedding gowns, veils, tiaras, gloves, purses, ring-bearer pillows, cake toppers and party favors. And at weddings, you'll notice that pearls have become essential jewelry for both the bride and bridesmaids.

Pearls of Wisdom from a Wedding Expert

Jet Taylor of J Taylor Bridal Jewels in Charlotte, North Carolina has advised brides for years on their wedding attire. Here are some of her tips on selecting wedding pearls:

- The bride's pearl jewelry should be well matched. For example, her pearl earrings should be of the same type and color as her pearl necklace. The bride is the featured attraction, so she should expect that her guests will be closely examining everything she's wearing on this special day.

- Pearl jewelry should be color-coordinated with the pearls on the gown rather than with the gown itself. For example, if the gown is ivory-colored and the pearls on it are white, the bride's pearl jewelry should also be white. The pearls on the gown should be the same color as those on the veil. In sum, all the pearls the bride is wearing should look like they were made to go together.

- If the bride would like to wear a necklace, earrings or brooch from her grandmother that doesn't match her other pearls, consider placing a note in the program stating the bride is wearing, for example, a pearl necklace in honor of her grandmother.

- If a bride or bridesmaid is wearing a necklace, it should be at least one inch above the neckline so it will not look as if it is going to fall into the dress. If the necklace is longer, it should be at least two inches below the neckline so that it will show and the necklace cannot fall into the dress

- Despite the above tips, the bride should remember that this is her day and she has a right to wear whatever she wishes.

How Lighting Affects Color

Just as luster is affected by lighting, so is color, but in a different way. If you were to take a photograph indoors under a light bulb with daylight film, the picture would be orangy or yellowish. If you took it under fluorescent light, the picture would look greenish. Even though, unlike cameras, your eyes can adjust to changes of color from lighting, you're still influenced by them. Consequently, your perception of pearl color will depend on the lighting under which the pearls are viewed.

The whitest, most neutral light is at midday. Besides adding the least amount of color, this light makes it easier to see various nuances of color. Consequently, you should judge pearl color under a daylight-equivalent light. Neutral fluorescent bulbs approximate this ideal, but some of these lights are better than others. Five recommendations are the Verilux Full Spectrum, Dazor Full Spectrum, Duro-Test Vita light, GE Chroma 50, and the Sylvania Design 50. This light from these sources, however, is still not as effective as true sunlight for seeing detail. For example, it's normally easier to read very fine print in sunlight than in artificial light. The intensity of the light from the sun has a lot to do with this.

When you shop for pearls, your choice of lighting will probably be limited. Use the information below to help you compensate for improper lighting.

Type of Lighting	Effect of Lighting on Pearl Color
Sunlight	Depends on the time of day, season of the year, and geographic location. At midday it normally has a neutral effect on the hue. Earlier and later in the day, it adds red, orange or yellow, so the pearls may look more pink or yellower.
Incandescent light bulbs, halogen spotlights and candlelight	Add red. Pearls may look more pink or yellowish.
Fluorescent lights	Depends on what type they are. Most intensify blue colors. Warm white tubes add yellow.
Light under an overcast sky or in the shade	Adds blue and gray, so pearls may look grayish or a bit bluish.

Emphasis on proper lighting when viewing gems has not been restricted to modern-day times. In 1908, in *The Book of the Pearl* (p. 370), Kunz and Stevenson wrote:

"At great receptions, large and apparently magnificent pearls are frequently seen, which are really of inferior quality, and yet owing to the absence of pure daylight, they can easily be mistaken for perfect specimens by any one not especially familiar with pearls. Indeed, if the royalties of Europe should wear all the pearls belonging to the crown jewels at the same time, in a palace or hall lighted with candles, gas, or even with some types of electric light, they would seem to have a quality which many of them do not and never did possess. It is, therefore, essential for the buyer to use every precaution in reference to the light in which he examines his purchase."

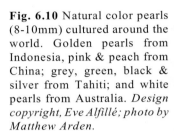

Fig. 6.10 Natural color pearls (8-10mm) cultured around the world. Golden pearls from Indonesia, pink & peach from China; grey, green, black & silver from Tahiti; and white pearls from Australia. *Design copyright, Eve Alfillé; photo by Matthew Arden.*

What Causes Pearl Color?

Many pearl farmers wish they had the full answer to this question. Then they could control the color of the pearls they cultivated. Now they have only partial answers or clues. Some of the determinants of pearl color seem to be:

● The type of host oyster. Oysters vary in their potential to produce certain colored pearls. For example, black pearls are cultivated in the black-lip oyster because other oysters don't produce pearls of the same type.

● The quality of the nacre. If the nacre is very thin, the color will look milky and lack overtone tints. Besides being affected by the number of layers of nacre, pearl color is affected by the thickness of each layer. In *Pearls of the World* (p. 71), researcher Koji Wada states, "The reason why the pearl made by the Akoya pearl-oyster has a better pink tone than pearls made by other mollusks is that it has layers of equal thickness."

● The environment in which they are grown. It's theorized that there may be trace elements in the water that affect the color. For example, cream-color pearls are typical of natural pearls from the Ohio River, but not of those found in other American rivers.

● The color of the tissue that is inserted with the bead nucleus. (Tissue from another oyster's mantle—the part of the oyster that secretes pearl nacre has to be implanted with the shell bead for a cultured pearl to grow). Pearl researcher Dr. Koji Wada has found that if the tissue inserted in Akoya oysters is yellow, cream-colored pearls tend to form. If white, white pearls result. Black pearl specialist and farmer Josh Humbert agrees. His Kamoka Pearls website says that the mantle of the donor oyster creates the eventual color of the pearl.

7

Judging Surface Quality

Imagine that you're buying a bouquet of roses for a special friend. If you were to look closely at each rose, you would probably notice some brown spots, small holes or torn edges. Yet it's doubtful that any of these flaws would keep you from getting the bouquet. You would select it on the basis of its overall attractiveness.

However, if you were buying just one rose for somebody, you would most likely examine it more closely and expect it to have fewer flaws than the roses in a bouquet. Judging pearls is much the same. Our standards of perfection for a single pearl are normally higher than for a strand. But whether we're dealing with roses or pearls, we should expect nature to leave some sort of autograph.

When discussing flaws in diamonds or colored gems, the jewelry trade uses the term **clarity**. This refers to the degree to which a stone is flawed. In the pearl industry, a variety of terms is used. For example:

Blemish	Spotting
Cleanliness or Cleanness	Surface quality
Complexion	Surface appearance
Flawlessness	Surface perfection
Purity	Texture

In the USA, **surface quality** or simply **surface** is the term most frequently selected to denote pearl clarity.

There are also many synonyms for the term "flaw." They include:

Blemish
Imperfection
Irregularity
Spot
Surface characteristic
Surface mark or marking

When dealing with diamonds and colored gems, gemologists limit the term "blemish" to surface flaws such as scratches and bumps. The term "inclusion" refers to flaws that extend below the surface such as cracks and holes.

"**Blemish**" takes on a different meaning when used with pearls. It means any kind of flaw, internal or external. This book often uses the term "flaw" because it's short and easily understood by the trade and general public. For the sake of variety, other terms are used as well.

Ironically, flaws can be positive features. They serve as identifying marks that indicate a gem is ours and not somebody else's. They help prove that it is real and not imitation. Flaws can lower the price of gems without affecting their overall beauty. Perfection does not seem to be a goal of nature. In fact, the longer a pearl is in an oyster, the more likely it is that irregularities will occur. Therefore, when shopping for pearls, there's no need to look for flawless ones; you just need to know which types of imperfections to avoid.

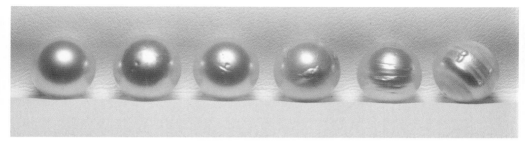

Fig. 7.1 Pearls ranging from clean to very heavily blemished *Photo © Renée Newman.*

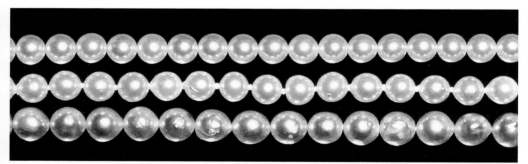

Fig. 7.2 Surface comparison photo. Top strand—relatively clean (unblemished), middle strand—moderately blemished, bottom strand—heavily blemished. *Photo © Renée Newman.*

Fig. 7.3 Enlarged view of same strands. *Photo © Renée Newman.*

Pearl Blemishes

A standardized terminology has not been developed for pearl blemishes. The terms found below are based primarily on those listed in the GIA (Gemological Institute of America) pearl grading course. These imperfections are usually judged without magnification.

- **Bumps and Welts:** Raised areas which are found alone or in groups. Sometimes they may even cover most of the surface area of the pearl. If bumps or welts are very large, they can put the pearl into the off-round category. Occasionally pearls have a wrinkled appearance. This is caused by groupings of welts.

- **Discolorations:** Spotty areas often caused from concentrations of conchiolin, a protein substance that holds nacre crystals together. Discolorations are not frequently seen because pearls are typically bleached to even out their color.

- **Chips, Gaps and Patches of Missing Nacre:** Blemishes which may occur on any type of pearl but that are particularly common on those with thin nacre.

- **Pits and Pinpoints:** Tiny holes on the surface which are normally hardly noticeable and, therefore, not serious. "Pinpoints" may also refer to tiny bumps since, from a distance, these look about the same as tiny pits.

- **Dimples:** Circular depressions or indentations which are often found in groups.

- **Dull Spots:** Areas of very low luster due to variations in nacre quality or contact with chemicals, cosmetics or skin secretions.

- **Cracks:** Breaks in the nacre and/or bead nucleus. Small cracks in the bead may look like little hairs trapped under the nacre. Cracks, even when not visible, can threaten the durability of a pearl.

- **Scratches:** Straight or crooked lines scraped on the pearl. These aren't serious unless the pearl is so badly scratched that the luster and beauty are affected.

Determining Which Blemishes Are Acceptable & Which Aren't

The presence of flaws isn't as important as the type, quantity and prominence of those flaws. Listed below are blemishes which would normally be considered unacceptable:

- **Cracks throughout the pearls**. Thick nacre does not crack easily; thin nacre does. Even if the cracks aren't noticeable, they are a sign that the nacre is too thin and that the pearls won't wear well over time.

- **Patches of missing nacre**. Just as diamonds with big chips are considered unacceptable, so are pearls with chunks of missing nacre. Both the beauty and durability of the pearl are affected.

- **Obvious discolorations throughout the pearls.** For the sake of beauty, try to select pearls with a uniform color. Plenty of them are available.

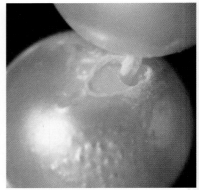

Fig. 7.4 Some typical pearl blemishes—pits, bumps, welts, holes, pinpoints and a dull white area. *Photo © Renée Newman.*

Fig. 7.5 Missing nacre around the drill hole. *Photo © Renée Newman.*

- **Prominent flaws on a single pearl**. When buying pearl earrings, pendants, pins or rings pay closer attention to the flaws. For example, a pearl with a large, visible bump would not be acceptable as the featured pearl of a jewelry piece, but it would be okay in a strand. If you are buying an expensive pearl and you want to compromise on price, try to select one whose imperfections can be hidden by the setting.

- **Blemishes which cover the majority of the pearl's surface.** They can direct a viewer's attention more to the blemishes than to the pearls themselves. Figures 7.6 and 7.7 are examples of how groups of minor flaws over a large surface area become more noticeable and therefore less acceptable.

Fig. 7.6 A group of minor pits

Fig. 7.7 A group of tiny welts

Despite the undesirability of blemishes, if you had to choose between heavily flawed, lustrous pearls and near flawless pearls with thin nacre and low luster, you'd be better off with the flawed pearls. At least you'd be getting some pearl for your money. Keep in mind when buying pearls that it's not just their inherent quality that determines their acceptability. Your needs and desires also count. If you're looking for a fine quality necklace, you'll want to avoid strands with noticeable flaws. If your budget is limited, you'll probably be glad that there are blemished pearls available at reduced prices. You have the final say as to what's acceptable and what's not.

Tips On Judging Surface Quality

When you shop for diamonds, salespeople may suggest that you look at the stone under magnification so you'll know its clarity. This won't happen when you shop for pearls. The reason jewelers don't have you view them under a microscope is because pearls are graded and valued based on how they look to the naked eye, not under magnification. Nacre thickness is an exception to this rule.

When dealing with knowledgeable salespeople who have your interests at heart, you won't have to look at pearls with a loupe (hand magnifier). They will point out the imperfections and other quality factors and show you how to compare pearls. But sometimes it's advisable to use a loupe, such as:

- **When dealing with people you don't know or who may not be trustworthy**. Suppose you are at a flea market or an antique show and you see a pearl piece you'd love to have that you would never find in a jewelry store. Or, suppose you are on vacation abroad and you want a souvenir but you don't know any jewelers and none have been recommended to you. In both cases, it would be advisable to use a loupe and check for flaws, thin nacre, dye and imitations. The more experienced you become at examining a pearl's surface and drill holes with a loupe, the easier it will be for you to identify pearls and judge their quality.

- **When the lighting is poor**. Suppose you're an antique dealer or a pawnbroker and you're in a place where the lighting is not ideal. And suppose you have to make a quick decision about whether to buy some pearls and how much to offer. Poor lighting will make it harder to judge surface quality and detect imitations. Use a loupe as a means of compensating for the lack of proper lighting.

- **Whenever pearls are being offered at a price that seems too good to be true.** There's usually a catch somewhere. It will probably be easier to find it with a loupe than with the unaided eye, especially for people who don't deal with pearls on a regular basis.

A few other pointers for judging imperfections are listed below:

- Besides looking at the pearls against a white background, look at them against a dark one. Certain flaws show up better against black or other dark colors. Also, hold the pearls in the air to examine them for flaws. Do not judge luster or color in this way, however.

- Roll the pearls; otherwise you may not see some serious flaws and you won't know what percentage of the pearls is flawed. An anecdote by Kunz & Stevenson in *The Book of the Pearl* (p. 371) illustrates the importance of looking at all sides of the pearls.

    A pearl necklace valued at $200,000, shown at one of our recent great expositions, was, to all appearances, a remarkably beautiful collection, and it was only when the intending purchaser took them from their velvet bed and held them in his hands that he realized that there was not a perfect pearl in the entire collection. It must have taken more than a week of study for the clever dealer to arrange them so that the best part, sometimes the only good part of each pearl, should be where the eye would fall upon it. After they had been turned in the hands a few seconds, not one perfect specimen was visible.

- Examine the pearls under a strong light. The more intense the light, the easier it is to see detail. When judging blemish, it's also a good idea to look at pearls under different types of lighting—bare/diffused, fluorescent/incandescent, close/distant. Each type may bring out different details in the pearls.

- Keep in mind that it's normal for pearls to have a few flaws.

Grading Surface Quality

The diamond industry has a standardized system for grading clarity based on a system developed by the GIA. Ten-power magnification is used. The advantage of having this system is that buyers can communicate what they want anywhere in the world. In addition, written appraisals and quality reports are more meaningful. The GIA has tried to establish such a system for pearls. As of 2010, their system defines four categories of surface quality:

- Clean—Pearl(s) is blemish-free or might have minute surface characteristics that are difficult to see

- Lightly spotted—Pearls have only minor surface irregularities visible

- Moderately spotted—Pearls show noticeable surface characteristics

- Heavily blemished—Pearls show obvious surface irregularities that might affect durability.

Most pearl dealers have their own systems for grading surface quality. Occasionally you'll come across grades such as AAA, AA, A. Depending on the supplier or store, these grades may refer to the luster, the flaws, a combination of these two factors, or they may include other factors such as shape and nacre thickness. In essence, pearl grades have no meaning except what the seller assigns to them. Therefore, do not rely on grades to compare pearl prices. Examine the pearls yourself, use your own judgment and consider the following:

- **The prominence of the blemishes**. Visible flaws away from drill holes are more serious than those near the holes. High bumps can be more noticeable than small pits or low bumps.

- **The type of flaws.** Chipped or missing nacre is usually more serious than bumps even though it may be less noticeable.

- **The percentage of the pearl surface that is flawed**. It's a lot more serious if 80% of the surface of a pearl is flawed than if only 10% of it is. You need to roll the pearls to check this factor.

- **The percentage of pearls on a strand that are flawed and to what degree**. This is a factor that doesn't exist in diamond grading. Pearl grading is more complex. It's much harder to develop consistent grades for sets of gems than for single gems.

8
Size, Weight, Length

Size

The size of round saltwater cultured pearls is expressed in terms of their diameter measured in millimeters. One millimeter is about 1/25 of an inch. Since pearl size varies within a strand, a range of ½ millimeter is usually indicated, e.g., 7–7 ½ mm. Occasionally, a few of the pearls might fall slightly above or below the size indicated. Usually the larger the size, the higher the price.

The size of non-round pearls can be expressed in terms of their greatest width and length and in some cases depth. The measurements are generally rounded to the nearest half or whole millimeter.

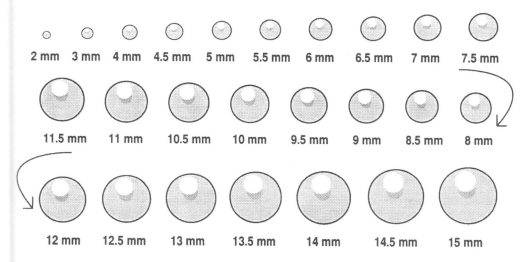

Fig. 8.1 Millimeter sizes. *Diagram by Dawn King.*

When determining the effect of size on price, keep in mind the following.

♦ Price jumps between pearl sizes are often uneven. As the sizes reach the 8 mm or 9 mm mark, pearl prices tend to jump more.

♦ Price/size relationships can vary from one dealer to another.

♦ The effect of size on price varies from one harvest to another. If too many pearls of one size are harvested, their price will go down.

♦ Demand can have an important impact on the way size affects price. If there's a high demand for a specific size, its price tends to increase. This explains why occasionally smaller pearls sell for more than bigger ones of the same quality.

Weight

When pearl wholesalers buy large lots of cultured pearls, they are often charged according to the weight of the pearls. The measure generally used is the **momme**, an ancient Japanese unit of weight which equals 3.75 grams or 18.75 carats. **Kan** is a Japanese unit of weight equaling 1000 momme. Pearls are not sold by the momme or kan in retail stores.

The size of natural pearls is often expressed in pearl grains. One **grain** equals 0.25 carat. Natural American freshwater pearls may be sold according to their carat weight. The **gram** is commonly used to express the weight of cultured freshwater pearls, although carat weight is also used. One **carat** = 1/5 gram. Or in other words 5 carats = 1 gram. Weight equivalences are summarized in Table 8.1. The approximate weight of individual loose pearls can be calculated by referring to both Tables 8.1 and 8.2.

Table 8.1 Weight Conversions

1 carat (ct)	= 0.2 g = 0.007 oz av = 4 p grains = 0.053 m
1 gram (g)	= 5 cts = 0.035 oz av = 20 p grains = 0.266 m
1 ounce avoirdupois (oz av)	= 28.3495 g = 141.75 cts = 565 p grains = 7.56 m
1 pearl grain (p grain)	= 0.05 g = 0.25 ct = 0.013 m = 0.0017 oz av
1 momme (m)	= 3.75 g = 18.75 cts = 75 p grains = 0.131 oz av

Table 8.2 (Based on data from the Shima Pearl Co)

Size	Pieces Per Momme	Size	Pieces Per Momme
2.5 mm	160 pcs	6.5 mm	9.3 pcs
3 mm	90 pcs	7 mm	7 pcs
3.5 mm	63 pcs	7.5 mm	6 pcs
4 mm	40 pcs	8 mm	5 pcs
4.5 mm	27 pcs	8.5 mm	4.2 pcs
5 mm	19 pcs	9 mm	3.5 pcs
5.5 mm	15 pcs	9.5 mm	3 pcs
6 mm	12 pcs	10 mm	2.5 pcs

Length

When pricing pearls, you should take into consideration the length of the strand as well as the millimeter size of the pearls. The pearl trade has specific names for different necklace lengths. They are as follows:

1. **Choker**   A 14–16 inch (35–40 cm) necklace whose central pearl normally lies in the hollow of the throat or just below it. It looks especially attractive with V-neck blouses and dresses.

2. Princess   A 16–20 inch (40–50 cm) necklace. This slightly longer length is well suited for pearl enhancers (detachable pendants) and can slenderize the neck.

3. Matinee   A 20–26 inch (50–66 cm) necklace. Some people like to wear a matinee length along with a choker. Or they have it strung with two hidden (mystery) clasps so it can also be worn as a bracelet and a shorter necklace.

4. Opera   A necklace about twice the size of a choker.

5. Rope   A necklace longer than an opera length. The defined length will vary according to the jeweler or company using the term.

Pearl necklace lengths are summarized in the following list:

1. Choker	14–16"	35–40 cm
2. Princess	16–20"	40–50 cm
3. Matinee	20–26"	50–66 cm
4. Opera	28–36"	70–90 cm
5. Rope	40" +	1 meter and longer

8.2 Courtesy Mikimoto Co.

The preceding lengths are approximate. Definitions of necklace-length terms can vary from one jeweler to another. Keep in mind that pearl strands become slightly longer (about 2 inches or 5 cm) when knotted and strung with a clasp to form a necklace. The following table will help you determine approximately how many pearls there are in a 14" and 16" strand.

There are some other terms relating to pearl necklaces that consumers might not be familiar with. They are:

Bib   A necklace of three or more concentric strands. The lowest strand normally does not fall below a matinee length.

Dog collar   A multi-strand choker-length necklace. The strands may be clasped together in a single clasp. "Dog collars" help conceal neck wrinkles.

Torsade   A multi-strand necklace formed by twisting strands around each other. This is a popular way to wear freshwater pearl strands.

Fig. 8.3 Dog-collar. *Photo from the Cultured Pearl Associations of America and Japan.*

Uniform strand   A strand whose pearls are all about the same size.

Graduated strand   A strand with pearls of different sizes which gradually get larger towards the center. Graduated strands provide a big pearl look at a lower price than uniform strands.

Table 8.3 (Based on data from the Shima Pearl Co.)

Size	Pearls per 14"	Pearls per 16"
2.5–3 mm	130	148
3–3.5 mm	110	125
3.5–4 mm	97	110
4–4.5 mm	83	95
4.5–5 mm	76	87
5–5.5 mm	70	80
5.5–6 mm	63	72
6–6.5 mm	57	65
6.5–7 mm	53	60
7–7.5 mm	50	57
7.5–8 mm	46	52
8–8.5 mm	43	49
8.5–9 mm	41	47
9–9.5 mm	39	44
9.5–10 mm	36	41

Strands with pearls over 10 mm (South Sea pearls) are usually longer than 16 inches.

9

Judging Make

Imagine spending fifteen years collecting more than 30,000 pearls just to find the right pearls for one necklace. Someone in Texas took the trouble to do this. The pearls on the strand had a variable fair to very good luster; most were round but some were off-round; they ranged in size from 3.70 mm to 8.15 mm; and their color ranged from brownish to purplish pink. That necklace could be classified as having an unusually fine make. Why? Because all of the pearls on the necklace were natural freshwater pearls recovered from lakes and rivers in West Texas. And it's amazing that so many pearls of this type could be so round and blend together so well. When judging make we have to take into account the availability of the pearls being graded.

Make is a combination of the following factors:
- How well the pearls match or blend together in terms of color, shape, luster, size and surface perfection
- How centered the drill holes are
- How seamless the transition of pearl size is in graduated strands

Make has a definite impact on price. Some dealers charge a premium that may range from 1%–15% for Akoya strands that are of very fine make. Others may discount them if the pearls don't match very well. Premiums of up to 30% or more can be charged for well-matched pairs of large, high quality natural or South Sea pearls. It can take a great deal of time and luck to find pearls that match.

Fine make is relative, though, and buyers should be flexible about their expectations. For example, one should not expect South Sea, freshwater or natural pearls to be as round and match as well as cultured Akoya pearls.

The definitions of what constitutes good, fair and poor make in Akoya pearl strands can vary from one dealer to another. Some may emphasize color, while uniform luster, size and/or shape may be more important to other dealers. All dealers, however, would probably agree that the overall appearance is what counts most when judging make. Figure 9.1–9.6 are examples of well-matched strands and earrings.

The Gemological Institute of America (GIA) uses the term **matching** to denote make. According to GIA guidelines "Matching describes the uniformity of pearls in jewelry. It is judged by the consistency of size, shape, color, luster, surface quality and luster quality. For pearls that are intentionally mismatched, harmonious design and balanced effect are also considered applicable factors."

As of 2010, the GIA pearl grading system lists the following matching categories:

Excellent: Most to all pearls have a uniform appearance and are drilled on-center.

Very good: Most to all pearls have only very minor variations in uniformity.

Good: Most to all pearls have only minor variations in uniformity.

Fair: Most to all pearls have noticeable variations in uniformity.

Poor: Most to all pearls have very noticeable variations in uniformity.

Not applicable: N/A is used when describing single pearls and certain intentionally mismatched items.

Fig. 9.1 Well-matched Domé Pearls® in earrings by Estevan Garcia. *Photo from the Latendresse family & American Pearl Co, Inc.*

Fig. 9.2 Well-matched American pearl earrings. *Design © by Eve J. Alfillé; photo by Matthew Arden.*

Fig. 9.3 Well-matched South Sea "twin" pearl drops. *Design © by Eve J. Alfillé; photo by Matthew Arden.*

Fig. 9.4 Well-matched Cortez Pearls® in earrings by TriGem Designs. *Photo: Colombia Gem House.*

Fig. 9.5 Well-matched freshwater pearl earrings from Inter World Trading. *Photo © Renée Newman.*

Fig. 9.6 Well-matched South Sea pearls from A & Z Pearls. *Photo by Diamond Graphics.*

As mentioned earlier, it's important to take into account the availability of the pearls being graded when judging make. This means that:

- Dyed and non-dyed strands should not be graded alike since it's a lot easier to match dyed pearls than those that aren't.

- Very-thick-nacre pearls shouldn't be discounted as much for shape variations as thin- and medium-nacre pearls since pearls that are in the oyster longer have a greater chance of growing irregular.

- Natural pearls should not be graded as strictly for make as cultured pearls.

Buyers should be careful not to become so concerned about perfect matching that they end up downplaying other quality factors. It's important to keep expectations realistic.

The author recalls being in Tokyo just after taking a pearl grading seminar. She looked at some of the highest priced Akoya strands in some of the most exclusive stores in Tokyo and was quite surprised to find not a single strand whose overtones matched. They all seemed to have a combination of green, pink and silver overtones, but the strands varied in the percentage of each color. Finally, she realized that she was being unrealistic and that as long as the body color looked uniform, the overtones blended together well and their differences weren't obvious, there was nothing wrong with the pearls.

Judging make requires a balanced perspective. On the one hand, we shouldn't be so lax that we let shoddy workmanship become the norm. On the other, we shouldn't be such perfectionists that no pearls can meet our standards. When you look at a strand of pearls, consider its overall impact. Your attention should not be drawn away by obviously mismatched pearls. Neither is it desirable for the pearls to be lackluster but perfectly matched. Look at as many different qualities and strands of pearls as often as possible. You will form a sense of what's acceptable and eventually you'll have an appreciation for what is truly fine make.

Fig. 10.1 A top quality Australian South Sea cultured pearl necklace (17-18.5mm) from A & Z pearls. *Photo by Diamond Graphics.*

Fig. 10.2 South Sea keshi cultured pearls. *Pearls and photo from the Pearl Exporting Company.*

10

South Sea Pearls (White & Yellow)

Mallory is puzzled. At the mall, she saw a large white pearl ring in a jewelry store window for $5000. Then, in another store window, she saw what appeared to be a ring of the same size and quality for $500. She went in and asked the salesman if it was a real pearl ring. He told her it was and suggested she try it on. She liked it, and considering the price of the other ring, she felt she was getting a bargain, and bought it. Now she is wondering why there was such a large difference in price between the two rings. Can you think of a possible explanation?

There is one. The pearl in the first ring was a whole **South Sea pearl**—a large whole pearl cultivated in a South Sea oyster. The pearl Mallory bought was a 3/4 **mabe pearl**—an assembled pearl, which was also probably from a South Sea oyster. A mabe pearl grows attached to the inner surface of the oyster shell. After it is cut from the shell, the nucleus bead which was inserted to make it grow is removed, and the remaining hole is filled with a paste or wax (and sometimes also a bead or colored plastic dome).Then it is usually covered with a mother-of-pearl backing although some bargain-priced mabes are backed with plastic. The resulting mabe pearl has a pearly nacre coating almost the same as a whole cultured pearl. The main difference is that it tends to be thinner. Consequently, some mabe pearls may crack very easily.

Even though the salesman was not wrong about the ring containing a real cultured pearl, he should have told Mallory it was an assembled pearl, especially since there is a vast price difference between mabe pearls and whole pearls. (Large fine-quality mabes are available for a few hundred dollars, whereas large fine-quality whole pearls can cost several thousand dollars each.)

Unfortunately, salespeople don't always disclose important information, and some sellers may not know the difference between a mabe pearl and a South Sea pearl. Moreover, some people in the trade do not even

Fig. 10.3 South Sea mabe pearl. *Photo © R. Newman.*

regard mabes as true pearls. No matter what their background is, salespeople should never call mabes South Sea pearls. Only a South Sea *whole* pearl merits the price and name of "South Sea Pearl."

Mabe pearls are commonly shaped like half pearls, which makes them ideal for pendants and pins. They are also grown in 3/4 shapes to make them appear more like whole pearls when set in mountings such as rings. If a mabe pearl is loose, it's easy to tell it's assembled because the mother-of-pearl backing has a different appearance than the pearl nacre (fig. 10.3). In addition, you can see the line where the backing and pearl dome were glued together. When mounted, however, a mabe pearl may look like a South Sea whole pearl or 3/4 pearl, particularly if the bottom of the pearl is encased in gold.

Assembled pearls may occasionally look like whole pearls. The winter 1989 issue of *Gems and Gemology* shows an assembled pearl which seemed to be a whole natural pearl when x-rayed (p 240). But when it was removed from its mounting, it became obvious that two pearl pieces had been glued together. The final GIA Gem Trade Laboratory report concluded "Assembled pearl consisting of two sections of natural pearl or blister pearls cemented together."

South Sea pearls are cultivated in a variety of places—Australia, Indonesia, the Philippines, Thailand and Burma (now called Myanmar). Currently, Indonesia is the most important producer of pearls in the 9 to 12 mm range. The main source of pearls over 12 mm has been Australia. Australia's first pearl farm was established in 1956 on the Northwest coast at Kuri Bay. Prior to that time, Australia was producing up to 75% of the world's supply of mother of pearl, and pearls were just sold as a byproduct.

The silver-lip (*Pinctada maxima*) oyster is the main oyster used in Australia to cultivate South Sea pearls. If it's healthy, it can produce up to four pearls inserted at different times. The cultivation period may range from 1 1/2 to 2 years. The oysters that are unsuitable for whole pearls or that reject the bead nucleus are used to culture mabe pearls. Most of the large white mabe assembled pearls sold today are cultivated in South Sea silver-lip oysters.

Gold-colored pearls are also very popular, but they are rare. The yellow-lip (also called gold-lip) oyster in which they are occasionally found, normally produces light yellow and cream-colored pearls. Indonesia is the main source of yellow pearls, but they are also produced in the Philippines and Thailand.

The most prized mabe pearls are cultivated in the Indo-Pacific *Pteria penguin* oyster, which is known for producing pearls with exceptionally fine luster and iridescence. Whole natural pearls are occasionally found in wild *Pteria penguin* oysters as well as in wild *Pinctada maxima* oysters (figs. 10.4 & 10.5).

Price Factors

South Sea pearls are priced according to their luster, color, shape, surface perfection, size and nacre thickness. But low price does not necessarily mean low quality when it comes to shape, color and size. The low price results from a greater supply and a lower demand of certain colors, shapes and sizes. Luster, nacre thickness and surface perfection, on the other hand, do affect the actual quality of pearls. Luster and nacre thickness are the most important of the price factors listed below:

LUSTER

The higher the luster, the more valuable the pearl. White South Sea pearls have a lower luster potential than Akoya pearls and Tahitian black pearls. Take this into consideration when evaluating white pearls. For tips on how to judge luster, see Chapter 5.

COLOR

As is the case with Akoya pearls, choice of color should be based on what will look best on the person who will wear the pearls.

Fig. 10.4 Rare natural South Sea pearls from the *Pteria penguin* oyster. *Pearls from the T. Stern Collection; photo by J. Grahl – Courtesy: Société Des Perles Fines.*

Fig. 10.5 A rare natural South Sea pearl from the *Pinctada maxima* oyster. *Pearl from the T. Stern Collection; photo by J. Grahl – Courtesy: Société Des Perles Fines.*

Fig. 10.6 South Sea pearl bracelet from Divina® Pearls. *Photo by Cristina Gregory.*

Fig. 10.7 White and golden South Sea cultured keshi. *Necklace and photo from Eliko Pearl.*

The color varies depending on which variety of *Pinctada maxima* oyster the pearl comes from—the silver-lip or gold-lip. The silver-lip oyster, the main oyster in Australia, tends to produce silvery white pearls. The gold-lip variety, which is more commonly found around countries such as Indonesia, Thailand and the Philippines, is more likely to produce yellow or cream-colored pearls.

The body color of South Sea pearls is judged similarly to Akoya pearls. Usually white pearls are more valued than yellowish and cream-colored pearls, but there is one major exception. Pearls with a natural strong pinkish-yellow color that dealers identify as **golden** can sell for as much as white pearls of the same size and quality. The more saturated the gold color, the more valuable the pearl, provided the color is natural. Figure 10.8 shows four South Sea pearls from the gold-lip oyster that have different yellowish or gold colors. The actual colors of these pearls is probably different. (Photographs do not show fine nuances of color accurately.) The presence of overtones and iridescence is very desirable in South Sea pearls. In white pearls, pink and silver overtones are more highly valued than bluish-gray and greenish overtones. Bluish overtones, however, are appreciated if they are combined with pink overtones.

When buying gold South Sea pearls, be sure to ask if the color is natural. A high percentage of them are dyed and/or irradiated, especially those with strong gold or grayish-gold colors. If the color is natural, have this written on the sales receipt. It's advisable, too, to have expensive pearls checked by a gem laboratory. Read Chapter 13—Pearl Treatments for a more detailed discussion of this topic.

Fig. 10.8 Natural-color yellow pearls from Indonesia. Their price decreases as the color becomes less saturated. Strong yellow colors that look golden sell for premium prices provided the color is natural. Light yellow and cream colors cost the least. *Pearls from King Plutarco, Inc. Photo © Renée Newman.*

SHAPE

The more round the pearl the more valuable it is. But round South Sea pearls are very rare, far more rare than Akoya pearls, which are smaller and have thinner nacre. The thicker nacre and longer growth periods of South Sea pearls leads to a wide variety of shapes. These cannot be described adequately with just the four Akoya shape categories of round, off-round, semi-baroque and baroque. For a description of other South Sea pearl shapes, see Chapter 4 and figure10.10. No matter what their shape, South Sea pearls are generally sold undrilled if they are not on a strand. This allows the buyer to determine how the pearls will be used or mounted. Be willing to compromise on shape. This may be necessary because of the high price and limited availability of round South Sea pearls.

Fig. 10.9 South Sea baroque pearls ranging in size from 14–18 mm. *Jewelry and photo from King Plutarco Inc..*

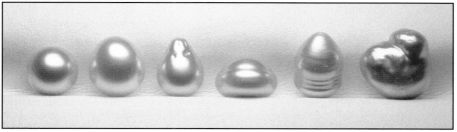

Fig. 10.10 Some South Sea pearl shapes, right to left: round, oval, drop, button, circle, baroque. These general categories don't always give a clear visual image of shape. A better description of the circled pearl shape might be circled bullet or circled drop. *Pearls from King Plutarco, Inc. Photo © Renée Newman.*

SIZE

South Sea pearls generally range in size from 9 to 19 mm. The size of semi-round pearls is indicated by the average diameter or by the smallest measurement of the diameter. The size of baroque pearls is most accurately represented by stating the length, width and height. However, sometimes only the two largest measurements are given.

When the Fourth Edition of this book was published in 2004, the world's largest round South Sea pearl was 24 mm. There may be larger ones now. Baroque pearls can have greater length measurements than round ones. As would be expected, the larger the pearl, the greater its value.

Fig. 10.11 South Sea pearls. *Earrings & photo from King Plutarco.*

Fig. 10.12 Two 17 mm South Sea pearls inlaid with Australian opal and fire opal. *Magic Pearl jewelry by Gabriele Weinmann; photo from Caricia Jewels Berlin.*

Fig. 10.14 South Sea pearls. *Earrings and photo from King Plutarco, Inc.*

Fig. 10.13 Golden South Sea pearl pendant and earrings from Divina Pearls. *Photo by Cristina Gregory.*

Fig. 10.15 Golden pearls from Indonesia. *Jewelry & photo from Albert Asher South Sea Pearl Company.*

The size of a cultured pearl is primarily determined by the size of its bead nucleus. The bigger the oyster, the bigger bead it can accept and the bigger pearl it can grow. Consequently, small Japanese oysters which measure 4 inches (10 cm) across, produce smaller pearls than the silver or gold-lip oysters which can measure 12 inches (30 cm) across. Black-pearl oysters, which also produce white pearls, grow up to about 8 inches (20 cm) across and usually produce a pearl in between the size of the silver-lip and Akoya oysters.

South Sea pearl strands aren't normally sold in the same ½ mm increments as Akoya pearls. They're usually graduated with larger pearls in the center and smaller pearls on the ends. It's very difficult to find matched South Sea pearls of one size. In addition, it's not cost effective to place large pearls at the back of the neck where they aren't necessarily seen. Consequently, it's best to give a size range when asking for South Sea pearl strands—for example, 12–14 mm. The most typical Australian South Sea strand size is probably 11–13 or 14 mm. Dealers will create special strand layouts such as 12–13 mm or 14–15 mm on request. But these are costly, and a deposit may be required before the dealer will make up the strand.

NACRE THICKNESS

Big pearls do not necessarily have thick nacre. As with Akoya pearls, the nacre thickness of cultured South Sea pearls has decreased during the past 30 years. In the April 1971 issue of *Lapidary Journal*, Australian pearl farmer C. Denis George stated that a good cultured South Sea pearl had a nacre thickness double the radius of the bead nucleus. In other words, a 15-mm pearl had about a 5-mm nacre thickness and a nucleus whose radius is about 2.5 mm. If this standard were used today, it would be very hard to find a good South Sea pearl. Judging from standards published by black pearl producers, South Sea pearls today should have a nacre thickness of at least 1 mm of the radius. (See nacre thickness section in Chapter 11).

One millimeter may sound thick compared to the minimum standard this book suggests for Akoya pearls—0.35 mm. Keep in mind that Akoya pearls have a finer-grained nacre than South Sea pearls and they are smaller. A 0.5-mm thickness on a 6-mm Akoya pearl is 1/6 of the radius. A 1-mm thickness on a 12-mm South Sea pearl is also 1/6 of the radius. Therefore, it's reasonable for buyers to expect nacre at least 1 mm thick on their South Sea pearls, especially considering their high cost.

Thin nacre is not as easily detected in South Sea pearls as it is in Akoya pearls. Because of the thicker nacre, the shell layers of the bead do not show up as well and it's harder to see the bead nucleus through the drill hole. In addition, the pearls are often mounted in jewelry so the drill holes aren't visible. Experienced dealers can often detect thin nacre by evaluating the quality of the luster. Thin nacre pearls may have a shiny surface, but they won't have a deep lustrous glow.

To avoid buying South Sea pearls with nacre that's too thin, you should select pearls with a good luster and deal with jewelers who consider nacre thickness important. It's also a good idea to have the pearls x-rayed by a gem lab when the price of the pearls is high enough to warrant the cost of an x-ray report, which is about $100 to $300. The nacre thickness can be measured in the x-ray photograph.

Like all other pearls, those from the South Seas come in a wide range of qualities and prices. Some sell for more than $5,000 and some sell for $50. The price factors above are what determine the value. For example, just take a $5,000 dollar South Sea pearl, make it smaller, add lots of flaws, give it a baroque shape, color it yellow, and give it a dull, drab luster. What can be the result? A $50 South Sea pearl.

Fig. 11.1 Tahitian cultured pearl. *Ring and photo by Chi Galatea Huynh of Galatea.*

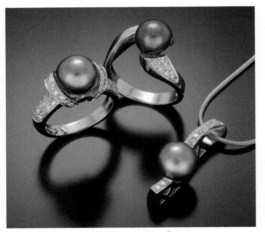

Fig. 11.3 Cultured Cortez Pearl® rings by Trigem Designs. *Photo from Columbia Gem House.*

Fig. 11.4 A natural black pearl from the *Atrina vexillum* scallop. *Pearl from the T. Stern Collection; photo by J. Grahl – Courtesy: Société Des Perles Fines.*

Fig. 11.2 Natural black pearls from the rainbow lipped oyster in the Gulf of California. *Pearls and photo from Pacific Coast Pearls.*

Fig. 11.5 Natural nacreous penn pearls from the *Atrina rigida* scallop. *Earrings from Pacific Coast Pearls; photo by Gwendolyn Rankin.*

11

Black Pearls

Black pearls are not necessarily black. More often than not they range from a light to very dark gray, but they may also look green, pink, lavender, blue or brown. It's the oyster source, not color, that determines if pearls are called black pearls. "Black pearl" is a generic term that refers to pearls from:

- Black-lipped pearl oysters (*Pinctada margaritifera*), Western to Central Pacific & Indian Oceans

- La Paz pearl oysters (*Pinctada mazatlanica*), Eastern Pacific between Baja California & Peru

- Rainbow-lipped (western-winged) pearl oysters (*Pteria sterna*), Eastern Pacific between Baja California & Peru

- Scallop pearls from the penn shell (*Atrina rigida*) or black pin shell (*Atrina vexillum*), also called *pinna nigra* or pinna nigrina. The pearls may be either nacreous or non nacreous. Atrina mollusks are found in various areas including the Indo Pacific, Gulf of California, Mediterranean and Atlantic Coast.

Some people mistakenly identify all black pearls as Tahitian pearls. Tahitian pearls are found in French Polynesia and they're marketed in Tahiti. Pearls from the Cook Islands are Cook Island pearls, not Tahitian pearls. Black pearls from the Gulf of California can be called La Paz pearls, Mexican pearls, Baja California pearls or simply black pearls. Some sellers call black pearls from the rainbow-lipped oyster "rainbow pearls" because of their natural rainbow-like colors. Baja pearls from the *Atrina rigida* mollusk are called penn or pen pearls.

If you go to Hong Kong, you may see strands labeled "black pearls" that sell for a couple hundred dollars. They are probably artificially colored Akoya pearls whose natural color was undesirable. In Tahiti, **"black pearls"** must be of natural color to merit the name of "black pearl" or "Tahitian pearl." The jewelers in both locations are correct in their use of the term "black pearl" as long as the treated pearls are identified as dyed, irradiated or treated black pearls. In other words, the unmodified term "black pearl" implies the pearl is of natural color.

Most of the black pearls sold on the market today are cultured. So for the sake of brevity, this book often omits the term "cultured" when referring to cultured black pearls. Nowadays, when pearls are natural (not created with human intervention), they are identified as such. Some natural black pearls are found in the rainbow lipped (*Pteria sterna)* oyster off of Baja California (fig. 11.2). Pearls from the *Pteria sterna* oyster are also being cultured in Bacochibampo Bay in the Sea of Cortez near the city of Guaymas and marketed by Columbia Gem House under the trade name Cortez Pearls® (fig.11.3) These pearls have a distinctive red fluorescence under long-wave ultraviolet light, which distinguishes them from Tahitian cultured pearls.

Scallop pearls from the black pin shell (*Atrina vexillum*) and the penn shell (*Atrina rigida*) are natural (figs. 11.4 & 11.5) The nacreous penn pearls from the Gulf of California are predominately black or grey with varying overtones such as green, magenta, blue, purple, lavander etc. The non-nacrous penn pearls from the Gulf of California can be green, brown, yellow, orange, or black, and tend to crack because they are mostly protein. Natural pearls of any color and from any mollusk are rare.

Fig. 11.6 Tahitian cultured pearls of natural color. *Necklace and photo from King Plutarco, Inc.*

Fig. 11.7 Note the distinctive red fluorescence under long-wave fluorescent lighting, which distinguishes the cultured Pteria sterna Cortez Pearl® at the far right from other pearls. Douglas McLaurin Moreno, the photographer, says that both natural and cultured *Pteria sterna* pearls react with the same red-pink fluorescence, but natural pearls seem to have a stronger fluorescence. Also, the lighter the color of the pearl is, the weaker the fluorescence is (light pink)... darker colored pearls display a blood-red fluorescence. *Pearls courtesy Columbia Gem House.*

Fig. 11.8 Same pearls viewed without long-wave fluorescent lighting. (From left to right): Black (dyed) Chinese FWP; White SSP; Japanese Akoya; Artificial-Black (silver nitrate) Akoya; Tahitian Black Pearl; Mexican Black Pearl (*Pinctada mazatlanica*) and the last one is a Cortez Pearl (from *Pteria sterna*.) *Pearls courtesy Columbia Gem House; photo by Douglas Moreno.*

Natural color black pearls can be confused with natural color "blue pearls." Unlike black pearls, whose color is an inherent characteristic of the pearl nacre, **blue pearls** derive their color from foreign contaminants in the nacre itself or between the nacre and the shell bead nucleus.

Naturally-colored dark Akoya pearls are good examples of blue pearls. They may be blue, black, gray or brown. Black pearls and blue pearls can look the same but because of the difference in the origin of their color, blue pearls are worth less. The fact that blue pearls might decay or lose their color if holes are drilled through them is another reason for their lower value.

Since there can be a great value difference between black pearls, blue pearls and artificially colored pearls even though they may look the same, consumers need to be concerned about buying black pearls that are misrepresented. In Chapter 13, you'll see how to spot pearls that are not true black pearls. Keep in mind, though, that the only sure way to identify a natural-color black pearl is to send it to a lab and have it tested.

Only within the last 30 to 35 years have cultured black pearls become commercially important. Most of them are cultivated in Tahiti (French Polynesia to be more accurate) and others are produced in places such as Okinawa, Fiji, the Cook Islands and Baja California.

Natural black pearls, however, became known in Europe after Hernando Cortez and later explorers discovered colored pearls in the Gulf of California. In the late 1700's and early 1800's, La Paz in Baja California became the black pearl center of the world. Natural black pearls in the South Seas were also being fished at this time. Gradually black pearls grew quite popular, especially among European royalty, such as Empress Eugenie of France. But the oyster beds were overfished and black pearls became scarce. Then in the 1940's, a large percentage of the black pearl oysters in the Gulf of California died for unknown reasons, which further depleted the supply. Fortunately, within the last 20 years, there has been a gradual redevelopment of black pearl fishing and culturing in the Gulf of California between Baja California and Mainland Mexico. As a result, a few natural pearls are now being found and cultured. Whole and mabe black pearls are being produced there.

Price Factors

Black pearls are priced according to their luster, color, shape, surface perfection, size and nacre thickness as follows:

LUSTER

Black pearls can look almost metallic. You should expect a higher and different luster from them than you would from white South Sea pearls. Dark nacre does not reflect light in the same way that white nacre does. The best way to learn the luster potential of a black pearl is to look at some black pearls ranging from very low to very high in luster. After you compare them, you probably won't be satisfied with a black pearl of low luster, and you shouldn't be. Good luster is an essential ingredient for pearl beauty. Keep in mind that lighting can affect black pearls in the same way it does white pearls, so compare pearls under equivalent lighting conditions. (See Chapter 5 for a discussion of lighting.)

Fig. 11.10 Tahitian pearl pendant by Anita Selinger. *Photo: Ralph Gabriner.*

Fig. 11.9 Multicolored Tahitian pearl necklace and bracelet. It was purchased for Elizabeth Taylor. *Jewelry by Erica Courtney; photo by Ralph Gabriner.*

Fig. 11.11 Tahitian cultured pearl. *Men's pendant from A & Z Pearls; photo by Diamond Graphics.*

Fig. 11.12 Black mother of pearl and diamond studded freshwater pearl. *Pendant and photo by Chi Galatea Huynh of Galatea Jewelry by Artist.*

Low luster in black pearls is often correlated with thin nacre, as is the case with white pearls. But thin-nacre black pearls can have good luster and thick-nacre pearls may have low luster. Consequently, it's best to treat luster and nacre thickness as two separate value factors.

COLOR

Twenty years ago, the preferred coloration for black pearls was dark gray with green and pink overtones (peacock colored). Today, however, tastes have changed. Lighter colored black pearls have become very popular and so have multicolored necklaces. Today, there's not much difference in price between dark "peacock-colored" pearls and the pastel-colored pearls. Brownish colors, however, are not as highly valued and neither are solid black pearls with no overtone colors.

Other overtone colors on black pearls are blue, gold, silver and a reddish purple called "aubergine," which is the French word for eggplant. Overtones may be present in a variety of combinations such as pink and green, and they are considered a plus factor. It's easiest to see the overtone colors in black pearls when the lighting is diffused and at a distance from the pearl. Bare lights close-up (e.g., ½ meter away) tend to mask the overtones in black pearls even though they bring out the overtones of white pearls.

There is no standardized system throughout the pearl industry for classifying or valuing the color of black pearls, and considering the complexity of it, there may never be. At any rate, you should select colors that you like and that look good on you.

SHAPE

Round and semi-round shapes are the most expensive. Drop shapes are the next most expensive followed by button shapes which are flat on one side and rounded on the other. The more symmetrical these shapes are, the more their value. Baroque shapes and circled pearls with ring-like formations around them are the least expensive. See Chapter 4 for a more detailed explanation of South Sea pearl shapes.

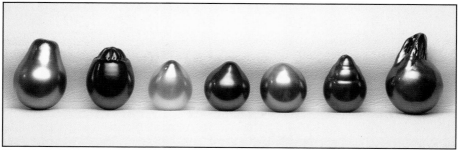

Fig. 11.13 Drops come in a wide range of shapes and sizes. The drops with the smoothest tops and most symmetrical form are usually priced the highest, all other factors being equal. Designers, however, often prefer unique, asymmetrical shapes. *Pearls from King Plutarco; photo: Newman.*

When you need to cut down on the price of a black pearl, shape is a good category on which to compromise. In fact, baroque and circled pearls often make more interesting jewelry pieces than round pearls do.

SIZE

Naturally the bigger the black pearl the more expensive it is. Black pearls generally range in size from about 9 to 18 mm with their average size tending to be between 9 and 11.5 mm. Some baroque black pearls may reach 25 to 30 mm in length. Size has a great impact on price. For example, a 1 mm increase in the size of medium-quality pearls can raise their price 100 to 200%.

At the retail level black pearls tend to be described and priced according to millimeter size. Weight may be used as an additional means of identifying them. This is the opposite of round diamonds where the price is based on the weight, but measurements may be given to help distinguish them from other diamonds of the same weight.

On the wholesale level large lots of black pearls are sold according to their weight, which is measured in momme (1 momme = 3.75 grams = 18.75 carats). The pearls are graded into various categories, and each category is assigned a per-momme price.

SURFACE PERFECTION

Flaws can decrease the price of black pearls considerably, which is an advantage for consumers. A black pearl can often be mounted in a way that will hide imperfections when worn. It can also be faceted to remove blemishes (fig. 11.14).

If you select pearl(s) with partially flawless surfaces, you can enjoy one or multiple clean-looking pearls for a lower price. Remember that blemishes on single pearls tend to be more obvious than on those in strands. It's normal for pearl strands to have some flaws.

Fig. 11.14 A 13.5 mm Tahitian faceted pearl ring by Mark Schneider. *Photo by John Parrish.*

NACRE THICKNESS

Black pearl nacre should be at least 1 mm (of the radius). The thicker the nacre the more valuable the pearl. As you are shopping, you may encounter salespeople who claim that all black or white pearls from the South Seas have thick nacre, and that nacre thickness need not be a consideration. Many people who specialize in producing or studying black pearls would disagree.

Dr. Jean-Paul Lintilhac, installer and developer of two black pearl farms in Tahiti, is one example. In his book, *Black Pearls of Tahiti*, he states that jewelers in Tahiti are worried about the thinness of the nacre of some of the pearls offered to them for sale. He explains that certain pearl farmers are in such a hurry to recover their investment that they harvest their pearls prematurely and as a result the nacre is very thin.

Fig. 11.15 Tahitian pearls. *Pendant from Divina Pearls; photo: Cristina Gregory.*

Fig. 11.16 Tahitian pearls. *Necklace from Divina Pearls; photo by Cristina Gregory.*

Fig. 11.17 Tahitian pearl men's pendant based on a carving of the old Polynesian God Kanaloa. Fishermen and water lovers look to him for protection. *Pendant and photo from Skinny Dog Design Group, Inc*

Fig. 11.18 Tahitian pearls. *Earrings and photo from Assael International.*

Fig. 11.19 Tahitian pearl (15.5 mm). *Design, ring and photo by Michael Saldivar.*

Fig. 11.20 Tahitian pearl (17 mm). *Design, ring and photo by Michael Saldivar.*

On page 85 of *Black Pearls of Tahiti,* Lintilhac writes: "Formerly a big pearl meant a good thickness of nacre, but with the supergrafts used today, size is no guarantee. If you are buying a big expensive pearl, you have the right to ask for an x-ray of it which will enable you to see and measure the thickness of the layers of nacre surrounding the nucleus. One millimeter of nacre is a minimum for a good pearl."

Tahiti Pearls, a major black pearl company, also tells consumers in their book *The Magic of the Black Pearl*, that nacre thickness is a criterion used to judge black pearl quality. They indicate a 1 mm to 1.5 mm nacre thickness as an appropriate range for black pearls.

Hisada and Komatsu of the Mikimoto Co. put nacre thickness at the top of their list of pearl quality factors (*Pearls of the World* p. 90). They state: "Nacre thickness is a basic factor in judging the elegance of the pearl. Its beauty and durability depend on the thickness of the nacre, its quality and quantity."

The Mikimoto company, in their leaflet "The Art of Selecting Cultured Pearls," tells consumers: "For beautiful pearls the most important factors are luster and nacre thickness."

Chapter 5 gives guidelines on determining if the nacre thickness of Akoya pearls is acceptable. Unfortunately these techniques do not work as well on black pearls. It's often impossible to see into their drill holes because the pearls may be glued to a jewelry piece such as a ring or pendant mounting. Also the nacre of black pearls may mask the layers of a shell bead nucleus that might be visible in a thin-nacre Akoya pearl. Dealers use luster as a guide to nacre thickness because a good deep luster typically signals good nacre thickness.

Usually the best way to determine the nacre thickness of a black pearl is with an x-ray. Thus, if you are spending thousands of dollars on a pearl piece, it's well worth your money to have a gem lab x-ray the piece to check for nacre thickness and to determine if the color is natural. But what should you do if you are paying, say $500 for a black pearl pendant? An x-ray in a case like that probably is not worth the money. The best thing you can do is to choose pearls with as high of a luster as possible and **buy your pearls from ethical jewelers who consider nacre thickness important.**

It's often hard to understand why one pearl may cost $50, for example, and another may cost $500. But let's consider how the preceding factors might work together to lower the price. If a pearl costing $500 decreases a little in size, its price may drop 50%, to $250. Going from a very high to very low luster could make its price drop another 50% to $125. If that pearl acquired lots of flaws, its price could drop even further— down to $50 or less.

Pearl pricing is not as mathematically precise as portrayed in the example above; nevertheless, the quality factors discussed can have a similar effect on any given pearl's price. It therefore pays to consider those factors as you shop and compare prices. When you look at pearl prices in ads and catalogues, remember, too, that they are meaningless if an adequate description of the pearls isn't included.

12

Freshwater Pearls

The general term for any bead or non-bead cultured pearl cultivated in a lake, pond or river area is **freshwater cultured pearl**. If a shell bead has been implanted into it along with a graft of mantle tissue, the resulting pearl is called a **bead-cultured** or **bead-nucleated freshwater pearl**. (The bead can be any shape; it isn't necessarily round.) For the sake of brevity, this book often omits the word "cultured" since practically all pearls today are cultured. Pearls that grow attached to the inner surface of an oyster or mussel shell are called **blister pearls**. If the pearls are not attached to the shell but grow within the mollusk, they are considered to be **whole pearls**.

The Chinese cultivated freshwater blister pearls in the shape of Buddha as far back as the thirteenth century. However, the Japanese, at Lake Biwa, are credited with being the first to succeed in cultivating whole freshwater pearls on a commercial basis. The technical roots of cultivating whole freshwater pearls are attributed to Masayo Fujita, the "father of freshwater pearl cultivation" (page 136, *Pearls of the World,* article by Hidemi Takashima, a chief engineer at the Nippon Institute for Scientific Research on Pearls).

Biwa pearls were first harvested in August 1925 and they had a shell bead nucleus like Akoya pearls. By the 1930's they were being sold overseas. Some merchants from India would buy these Lake Biwa pearls from Fujita and then resell them to the Middle East as highly valuable Persian pearls for huge sums of money.

Later, freshwater pearls were produced by simply inserting into the mollusk a small graft of living mantle tissue (a membranous tissue which secretes nacre and lines the inner shell surface of mollusks). Mantle cells can form a small pocket in which they continue to secrete pearl nacre. The pocket is called a **pearl sac**, and grows with time by cell division; in this way the pearl grows also. Pearl farmers noticed that after the first harvest, mussels can spontaneously grow pearls a second and third time in the pearl sacs. However, the second-generation pearls are flatter and not as plump as the first pearls the mussel produces.

Pearls that are cultivated using just mantle tissue have been called **tissue-nucleated pearls** in America and **non-nucleated** pearls in Europe. As of February 16, 2010, the World Jewelry Federation has authorized the term "keshi" as "a trade term that designates a non-beaded cultured pearl formed accidentally or intentionally by human intervention in marine pearl oysters such as the Akoya oyster, Silver/Gold lipped oyster, Black lipped oyster and freshwater molluscs." Labs in Europe and America, however, call them **non-bead cultured pearls** on their pearl reports.

Today, most freshwater pearls are produced in China, and most are non-bead cultured because it's easier to train people to produce them. However, the production of a bead cultured freshwater pearls is increasing.

One popular method of bead nucleation involves implanting a coin-shaped nucleus and tissue graft in the mantle of a mussel and leaving it there for one to four years to form a coin pearl. If the coin pearl is harvested in one year, the mussel can be returned to the water. Within the empty pearl sac of the coin pearl, another pearl may be spontaneously produced. It's usually a flatter petal-shaped pearl, which is called a **keshi, petal pearl or second-generation pearl**. If a pearl farmer prefers to grow another bead-nucleated pearl, he can have the first-generation coin pearl removed and replaced with a round bead in the same pearl sac. In another one or two years, another pearl with the round bead nucleus is produced. It will typically have a tail and resemble a flame. Consequently the second pearl with the round nucleus is often called a **flame pearl** or **fireball**. This is an oversimplification of freshwater pearl cultivation, which is explained more thoroughly and accurately in the Summer 2007 issue of *Gems & Gemology,* pp 138-145, "Continuity and Change in Chinese Freshwater Pearl Culture," by Doug Fiske and Jeremy Shepherd.

A second and older form of bead nucleation involves implanting a piece of mantle tissue and nucleus directly into the body of the mussel. Instead of being placed in the mantle tissue, the bead is placed among the organs of the mussel, usually the gonads. This is the same method used to cultivate saltwater and Japanese Biwa nucleated pearls and it's surgically more demanding than the method used for cultivating flame pearls. Fuji Voll of Pacific Pearls calls this type of bead cultured Chinese pearl an **in-body bead-nucleated pearl.** Voll has some very large, semi-baroque Chinese freshwater pearls that he says are probably in-body bead-nucleated pearls. He says these pearls tend to have a textured surface if they're baroque shaped, whereas flame pearls generally have fluid shapes and a smoother surface.

In January 2010, Jack Lynch of Sea Hunt Pearls announced a new type of Chinese freshwater pearl, which is nucleated with a dried hard piece of pond mud. As the pearl is forming, water seeps into the area with the nucleus and dissolves the hardened mud. When the pearl is drilled, a liquid drains out from the pearl leaving a hollow area. The walls of the pearl are very thick and stable. Fuji Voll calls this method of culturing freshwater pearls, a lost nucleus method. The large lightweight pearls are ideal for earrings. These pearls, which Lynch calls souffle pearls, were available for sale at the 2010 Tucson Gem Show.

The quality of Chinese freshwater pearls has steadily improved during the last two decades and their sizes have been increasing as well. Ever since the 1990's, Chinese freshwater pearls have been sold as attractive low-cost alternatives to Akoya pearls. Today freshwater pearls are also sold as an alternative to South Sea pearls, and they are frequently combined with Tahitian and Australian pearls to create appealing multicolor strands. Ethical dealers disclose that these strands are a combination of both saltwater and freshwater pearls.

China and Japan are not the only places where freshwater pearls are found. Europe has been a source of natural freshwater pearls. Some Scottish pearls are shown in figure 12.8. Overfishing, flooding and pollution have either decreased or, in some areas, eliminated the supply of these natural pearls.

Whole and blister freshwater pearls with a shell bead nucleus have been cultivated in the United States in Tennessee. Unlike most other freshwater pearls, American cultured pearls are never bleached, dyed or treated. You'll find them in a wide variety of shapes including marquises, drops, coins, tadpoles, domes and bars. Tennessee is also known as the primary source of the shell bead nuclei in Akoya and South Sea pearls.

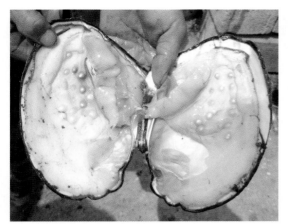

Fig. 12.1 First view of non-bead cultured freshwater pearls when mussel is opened. *Pearls & shell from Grace Pearl; photo © Renée Newman.*

Fig. 12.2 Same pearls viewed after removal from the mantle. *Photo © Renée Newman.*

Fig. 12.3 Close-up of five of the 33 pearls in fig. 12.2. Pearls from the same mussel and same harvest can have different shapes, sizes and natural colors. *Photo © Renée Newman.*

Fig. 12.4 Freshwater coin pearls of various shapes that were produced between 2000 and 2004. *Pearls and photo from Shogun Pearls.*

Fig. 12.5 Second-generation keshi-type pearls from Sea Hunt Pearls. *Photo by Lee-Carraher.*

Fig. 12.6 Left to right: Chinese hollow/lost-nucleus pearls, Chinese in-body bead-nucleated pearls, Japanese in-body bead-nucleated pearls, Chinese flame (fireball) bead-nucleated pearls. *Freshwater pearls from Pacific Pearls; photo © Renée Newman.*

Fig. 12.7 Lightweight coin pearls. These are cultivated by inserting pieces of plastic sheeting with large grafts of mantle tissue in a first operation. The broken pearl in the photo grew around a textured piece of plastic-like imitation leather. Unlike shell nuclei, thin bits of plastic contribute little to the weight of the pearl. This might be a reason why so many vendors call these lightweight-coin pearls non-nucleated. Lightweight coin pearls are a significant part of China freshwater pearl production. *Text by Fuji Voll; pearls from Pacific Pearls; photo by Marcia Fentress.*

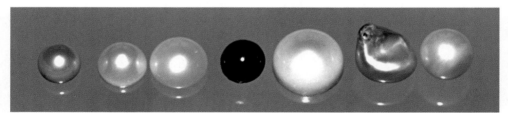

Fig. 12.8 Scottish natural river pearls from *Margaritifera margaritifera. Photo and pearls from Alan Hodgkinson.*

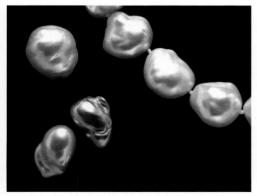

Fig. 12.9 Freshwater pearls (left) that look similar in size and shape to baroque South Sea pearls (right). *Photo and pearls from Eliko Pearl.*

Fig. 12.10 Chinese freshwater pearls that resemble Akoya pearls. *Photo and pearls from Eittige.*

Fig. 12.11 Chinese fw pearls harvested in 1978.

Fig. 12.12 Chinese fw rice pearls cultured in 1980's.

Fig. 12.13 Chinese fw pearls from the 1990's.

Fig. 12.11 One of the first strands of natural color pink freshwater pearls cultured in China (1978) and a neckpiece set with a tourmaline carved by Doug Klein. *Design by Fred & Kate Pearce, photo by Tommy Elder.*

Fig. 12.12 Rice-shaped freshwater pearls cultivated in China in the 1980's. *Necklace and earrings copyright Fred & Kate Pearce, photo by Tommy Elder.*

Fig. 12.13 Chinese freshwater pearls cultured in the early 1990's. *Design copyright by Fred & Kate Pearce; photo by Tommy Elder.*

Fig. 12.14 Natural-color 8–9 mm Cfw pearls from the early 2000's and neckpiece of drusy quartz carved by Dieter Lorenz. *Design © 2003 by Fred & Kate Pearce; photo by Ralph Gabriner.*

Fig. 12.15 Cultured Chinese freshwater pearls from the early 2000's, which are coin-shaped with tails. Top-drilling them is easier and creates a distinctive design. *Necklace from Pearlworks; photo by Azad.*

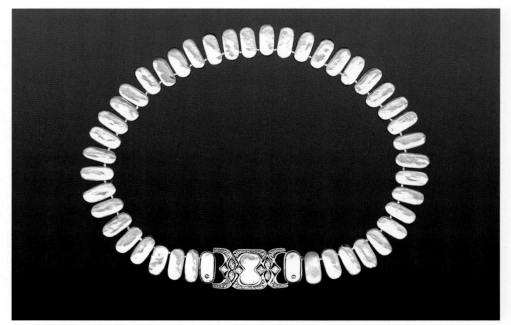

Fig. 12.16 Necklace of American freshwater pearls cultured before 2004 accented with a diamond and mother of pearl 18K gold clasp. *Jewelry design copyright by Eve J. Alfillé; photo by Matthew Arden.*

Fig. 12.17 Chinese 12.3–14,6 mm round bead-nucleated freshwater pearls cultivated after 2004. *Pearls from Sea Hunt Pearls; photo by Lee-Carraher*

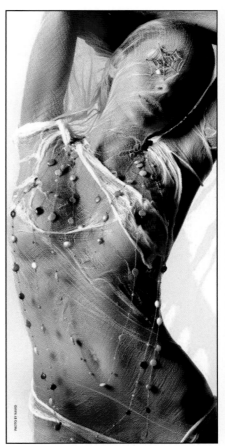

Fig. 12.18 Chinese freshwater pearl attire and photo from Eittige.

Fig. 12.19 Large Chinese freshwater pearls mixed with South Sea and Tahitian pearls. *Pearl from Sea Hunt Pearls; photo by Lee-Carraher.*

Fig. 12.20 Chinese freshwater pearl jewelry and photo from Eittige.

Price Factors

The grading of freshwater pearls is more variable than that of saltwater pearls. Nevertheless, there is agreement about certain value factors. Freshwater pearls are generally valued according to the following criteria:

LUSTER

The higher and more even the luster, the greater the value. Low-quality freshwater pearls may seem lustrous to a lay person because often part of their surface is very shiny. However, if some areas of the pearls look milky, chalky and dull, they are considered to have a low luster. In high-quality freshwater pearls, there is an evenly distributed luster and a high contrast between the light and dark areas of the pearls.

When judging freshwater pearls for luster, examine them on a white background and be sure to roll them so you can see their entire surface area. If possible, compare strands of different qualities. It's important that your eye become sensitive to luster variations because luster is one of the most important determinants of value in pearls of all types. For more information on judging pearl luster, see Chapter 5.

SMOOTHNESS

The smoother the pearl, the more valuable it is. Even though bumpy, wrinkled surfaces can lower the value of freshwater pearls, the bumps and wrinkles are not considered flaws. Consequently, this chapter treats smoothness as a separate category from surface perfection.

SIZE/WEIGHT

As a price factor, freshwater pearl size is not as important as luster and surface quality. Freshwater pearl prices are generally quoted by weight or by the strand. The gram is probably the most common unit of weight used at the retail level, but some dealers quote prices according to carat weight. Suppliers of large quantities of pearls may use the "momme" which equals 3.75 grams (18.75 carats).

The measurements of pearls are often listed along with their weight as an additional description and means of identification. The size of round freshwater pearls may be expressed by their diameter, measured in millimeters. Irregular pearls may be described using two or even three measurements; one of them should be the shortest that can be measured across the pearl.

The October 2009 issue of *Gems & Jewelry* showed an antique pearl which might be the largest freshwater pearl on record; it's 70 x 43 x 39 mm. On March 1, 2010, the G & G E-Brief reported receiving two near-round well-matched freshwater pearls that ranged from 17.05 to 17.67 mm in size.

SHAPE

Usually the more round a pearl is, the greater its value. Good symmetry, too, can make a shape more valuable. In addition, thin shapes tend to sell for less than fatter-looking shapes. Most freshwater pearls are baroque shaped. This is the lowest priced shape, all other factors being equal. Large high-quality, baroque shapes can command high prices and make distinctive jewelry pieces.

In 1992, many semi-round (off-round) and ovalish freshwater pearls became available. Some were described as **potato, corn** and **pea shapes**. Off-round pearls can be used to make impressive looking jewelry pieces that sell for moderate prices. A close-up view of off-round freshwater pearls is provided in figure 12.21.

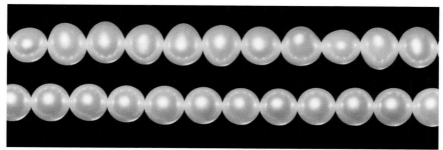

Fig. 12.21 Chinese freshwater strand (top). From a distance, it resembles a strand of round saltwater pearls (bottom). Off-round freshwater pearls may sell for 1/3 to 1/10 the price of saltwater pearls of similar size, luster, color and surface quality. *Photo © Renée Newman.*

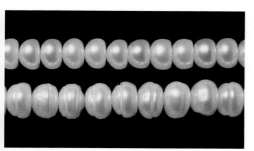

Fig. 12.22 Chinese freshwater pearls that resemble corn kernels. *Photo © Renée Newman.*

Fig. 12.23 Large baroque Chinese freshwater pearls with distinctive shapes. *Pearls from Inter World Trading. Photo © Renée Newman.*

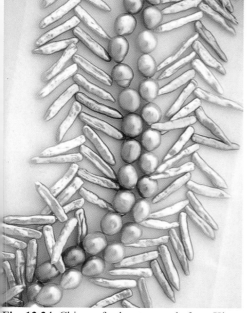

Fig. 12.24 Chinese freshwater pearls from Kings Ransom. *Photo by Betty Sue King.*

Fig. 12.25 Some of these dyed Chinese freshwater pearls resemble baroque Tahitian pearls in terms of shape and color. *Pearls from Kings Ransom; photo: Betty Sue King.*

Fig. 12.26 Chinese freshwater cultured pearl skirt. *Brooch by A & Z Pearls; photo by John Parrish.*

Fig. 12.27 Japanese Lake Biwa cultured pearl. Clown *brooch by A & Z Pearls; photo by John Parrish.*

Fig. 12.28 Caterpillar body—Chinese freshwater pearl; head—Tahitian black pearl; leaf—white Chinese freshwater keshi pearl. *Brooch by A & Z Pearls; photo by John Parrish.*

Fig. 12.29 American freshwater pearl pin/pendant by Fred & Kate Pearce. *Photo by Ralph Gabriner.*

Stick shapes are created by inserting long strips of mantle tissue in the mussel. Square, coin, diamond and rectangular shapes are made by inserting a shell nucleus with those shapes. Freshwater pearls also have a wide variety of baroque shapes thanks to their abundance of nacre (compared to saltwater pearls) and the high proportion of them without a bead nucleus.

SURFACE QUALITY

Obvious blemishes such as discolorations, pits and cavities can decrease the value of a pearl considerably, especially if the pearl is otherwise of high quality. Flaws in baroque shaped pearls tend to be less noticeable and therefore less consequential than those in smooth symmetrical pearls.

COLOR

Fresh water pearls come in a wide variety of body colors—white, pink, orange, yellow, lavender, gray. Some pearls are even bicolored. When you ask freshwater pearl dealers what are the most valued body colors, you get a variety of answers. Some price their white pearls higher, others place a higher value on certain colors such as pink and mauve, some raise the prices as the intensity of the colors increases, while other dealers price all the colors about the same. Since the color grading of freshwater pearls is so flexible, the best way to know how an individual pearl dealer prices color is to ask. Most freshwater pearl dealers would agree on the following:

- The body color does not affect the price of freshwater pearls as much as it does that of saltwater pearls.
- The presence of overtone colors such as pink and silver makes them more valuable.
- Iridescence (orient) increases the value of pearls. Iridescence and high luster are interrelated.
- Natural color pearls are more highly valued than those which are dyed and/or irradiated. Dark colors are most likely treated, but some factories treat lighter colors in order to strengthen them.

NACRE THICKNESS

Nacre thickness is usually not an issue in cultured freshwater pearls because most freshwater pearls do not have a shell nucleus. When one is present, the nacre is usually thicker than in Akoya pearls. One of the biggest selling points of freshwater pearls is that they usually have a higher percentage of pearl nacre than their saltwater counterparts.

Freshwater pearls typically cost less than saltwater pearls. Low prices, though, don't necessarily mean low quality. Some $20 strands of Chinese freshwater pearls have a better luster, more orient and a higher percentage of pearl nacre than the majority of the cultured saltwater pearls on the market today. Therefore, don't just judge pearls by their price tag. Consider their luster, their color, their uniqueness. If you do, you'll discover that freshwater pearls offer great variety, beauty and value.

13

Pearl Treatments

All pearls must be cleaned and washed to remove residues and odors. They are typically tumbled in rotating barrels with salt during this procedure. The tumbling must be closely monitored; otherwise, some of the nacre may wear off. There are other processes which are not considered routine and which should therefore be disclosed. Some of these are listed below.

Bleaching: Chinese freshwater pearls and Akoya pearls are often bleached with chemicals. This whitens them and makes the color look more even. Improper bleaching can soften the nacre and make it more susceptible to wear, especially if the nacre is thin. Top quality pearls do not need to be bleached, and it would be pointless to possibly reduce their luster and durability by treating them. American freshwater pearls, black pearls and light colored South Sea pearls normally are not bleached. However, this is changing with white South Sea pearls because some are now undergoing chemical bleaching. Tahitian pearls may be bleached to make them look brown; these are sold as "chocolate pearls."

Buffing: This is done to improve luster and remove superficial scratches. Beeswax or chemical polishes are sometimes used during buffing to add luster. The wax wears off fast and the chemicals may eat away the nacre. Buffing without chemical intervention is considered acceptable if it's done to clean off oil and dirt from the pearl and remove minor scratches.

Coating: There have been reports of pearls being coated with lacquer in order to temporarily improve luster, but it's difficult to find samples. Good-quality pearls do not have to be coated to look lustrous. In a few instances, pearls have been darkened with thin plastic coatings to make them look like Tahitian pearls. This coating can be easily detected by its strange feel and by bald spots on the pearl where the coating may have worn away. Coating pearls in this manner is not an accepted trade practice.

Filling: Low-quality cultured baroque pearls are occasionally filled with an epoxy substance if they are partially hollow or have a loose nucleus. This helps the bead nucleus stay in position when the pearls are restrung; it makes the pearls more solid and improves their durability.

"Hollow natural pearls are often filled with foreign materials to bring them to somewhere near the weight one would expect for a pearl of that size," reports Stephen J. Kennedy of the Gem Testing Laboratory of Great Britain. He provided this information with supporting photographs at the AGA Symposium '98 Seminar in Tucson, Arizona and in the January-March 1998 issue of the *Australian Gemmologist*. Natural pearls are often sold by weight, which can lead to this practice. Such fillings can be detected with x-radiographs.

Dyeing: Akoya pearls are often soaked in pink dye to give them a desirable pink tint. This dye can usually be detected in the drill holes or in cracks (13.1 & 13.2). Yellow and golden pearls may also be dyed (figs 13.3–13.5). These pearls are especially popular in Asia.

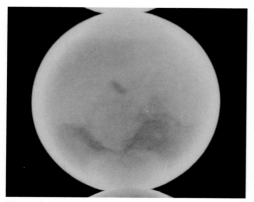

Fig. 13.1 Pink dye in pearl cracks. *Photo © Renée Newman.*

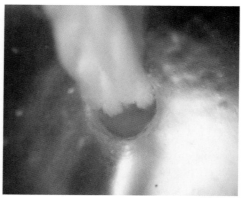

Fig. 13.2 Pink dye in pearl drill-hole. *Photo © Renée Newman.*

Fig. 13.3 High quality Akoya strands. Top: Natural color, unbleached strand; bottom, pinked strand. *Pearls and photo from Jeremy Shepherd at Pearl Paradise.*

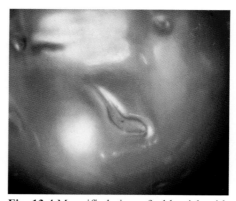

Fig. 13.4 Magnified view of a blemish with dye concentrations in a dyed golden South Sea pearl. *Photo © Renée Newman.*

Fig. 13.5 Dye concentrations and black nucleus visible in blemishes of two dyed pearls. *Photo © Renée Newman.*

Fig. 13.6 Visible dye concentrations. *Photo © Renée Newman.*

Shane Elen of the GIA Research Department wrote some excellent articles on identifying treated and untreated South Sea yellow pearls in *Gems & Gemology*: Summer 2001, Spring 2002 and Summer 2002. In some cases, it can be difficult and even impossible for gem labs to prove that yellow pearls are of natural color.

Off-color pearls from the Akoya and silver- or gold-lip oysters are sometimes darkened with dye to improve their appearance. They are then sold as "black pearls" or "chocolate pearls" depending on their color. If black pearls are smaller than 8 mm, just assume they are dyed Akoya pearls. Dyeing these small pearls is an accepted trade practice because it provides consumers with an option that is not available from natural-color Akoya pearls. Nevertheless, the treatment must be disclosed.

Light-colored pearls from the black-lip oyster are occasionally darkened. Many people associate the term "dyed" with the terms "cheap" and "fake." However, dyed black pearls were sold in fashionable stores as far back as the 1930's—long before black pearls were being commercially cultivated. Dyed black pearls were considered elegant then, and they are still in demand. Moreover, they are much more affordable than their naturally-colored counterparts.

If pearls are not properly dyed, the color won't be stable. Therefore, it's important to buy dyed pearls from reputable jewelers. That way if there is a problem, you'll be able to return the pearls and get a refund. If you're buying expensive *untreated* pearls, have them checked by an independent gem laboratory. Some are listed at the end of Chapter 15.

Irradiation: This method works best on freshwater pearls, but off-color Akoya and South Sea pearls may also be darkened in this manner. It involves bombarding pearls with gamma rays. This blackens the shell bead nucleus of Akoya and South Sea pearls and can make their nacre appear dark if it is thin. Sometimes pearls are both dyed and irradiated. The irradiation will give them an iridescent bluish or greenish gray color and the dye will further darken their appearance.

Silver salt treatment: This is the most common way of blackening Akoya pearls. The pearls are soaked in a weak solution of silver nitrate and diluted ammonia and then exposed to light or hydrogen sulfide gas. Unfortunately, the silver nitrate tends to weaken pearls and make them more susceptible to wear. Silver nitrate treatments can usually be detected by X-radiography.

Dying the bead nucleus: Occasionally shell bead nuclei are dyed before they are inserted in the oyster. Afterwards the dark bead may show through the nacre and make the pearl nacre look dark.

Injecting metal fluids into the pearl's sac. This is done during the culturing process to induce varying colors in a pearl, depending on the metal used.

Heating: Golden South Sea pearls are occasionally heated to intensify their color. High-tech lab equipment is required to detect the heating process.

Natural Color or Not?

As you can see, dyeing is not the only means of coloring pearls. However, for the sake of brevity, the term "**dyed**" will be used in the rest of this chapter to describe any artificially colored pearl.

Fig. 13.12 Tahitian black pearl solitaire of natural color and a smaller black dyed Akoya pearl in a three-pearl ring. Assume that black pearls less than 8 mm are dyed and/or irradiated. *Jewelry by Erica Courtney; photo by Ralph Gabriner.*

Fig. 13.13 Dyed freshwater pearls that were sold on an Internet site as a Tahitian pearl necklace for $25 including shipping. The low price, off-round shape, 7.5-mm size, and dye concentrations are clues that they're not Tahitian pearls. *Photo © R.enée Newman.*

Fig. 13.14 Natural-color brown Tahitian pearl from Kojima Company. *Photo by Sarah Canizzaro.*

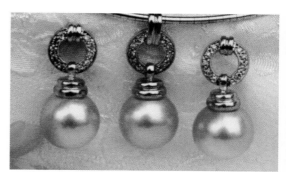

Fig. 13.15 Natural-color golden pearls with normal color variation. *Pendant & earrings from Divina Pearls; photo, Cristina Gregory.*

Fig. 13.16 Treated Tahitian chocolate pearls. *Jewelry & photo from King Plutarco, Inc.*

If you're interested in black pearls, look at many examples of them. Next look at dyed pearls and compare their color. Gradually, you'll get a sense of what the body colors and overtones of black pearls look like. People who work with black or yellow pearls on a regular basis can usually spot dyed pearls instantly. But even experts can be fooled. Therefore, when making a major purchase, have your pearls tested by an independent gem lab.

Magnifier Test: Examine the surface of the pearl with a 10-power magnifier (loupe). If the color in or around the blemishes is stronger and more intense than the rest of the pearl, this is a good sign the pearl is dyed. Absence of visible dye is not proof of natural color; not all blemishes of dyed pearls show dye.

Many appraisers, jewelers and gemology students use this book as a reference, and they're interested in some of the more technical ways of detecting dyed pearls. The following methods require special equipment and are not cost effective for the consumer.

Infrared Test: If you have a camera, you can photograph the pearls with color infrared film(Kodak, Ektachrome Infrared Film, IE 135-20). Naturally colored pearls tend to look blue, whereas pearls colored with silver salts generally look yellow (or range from greenish blue to yellow green). (Komatsu and Akamatsu, *Gems & Gemology*, Spring 1978).

Fiberoptic Test: If black pearls appear brownish under fiberoptic illumination but not under tungsten light bulbs, this suggests they were dyed with silver nitrate. Good quality, natural-color Tahitian pearls usually retain their normal colors under fiberoptic lights. Occasionally, low-grade, mottled Tahitian pearls look brownish. (Stephen Kennedy, *Australian Gemmologist*, January-March 1998, p.18.)

Fluorescence: The pearls are examined under long-wave UV radiation. Natural-color black pearls will generally have a fluorescence ranging from a bright red (pearls from Baja California) to a dull reddish brown (Tahitian pearls). Dyed pearls tend to show no reaction or else fluoresce a dull green. (See page 143 of the 1989 issue of *Gems & Gemology*, part of a good article on the Polynesian black pearl by Marisa Goebel and Dona Dirlam.)

Microscope: The pearls are viewed under a 100+-power microscope through crossed Polaroid lenses. If they exist, traces of the chemical coloring can be seen using this method. (Hisada and Komatsu, *Pearls of the World,* pp. 92-93).

X-radiograph: An x-ray photo called an **x-radiograph** is taken of the pearls. If the pearls are dyed with silver salts, a pale ring between the nacre and the shell bead nucleus can often be seen. In addition, there is less of a contrast between the bead and the nacre.

X-ray Fluorescence: The pearls are exposed to x-rays. Then the emitted wavelengths are measured with an instrument called a spectrometer to detect trace elements such as silver on the surface of the pearl.

As you can see, there are a wide variety of tests for identifying dyed pearls. Using a combination of the simple tests will help you spot obvious cases of dye, but when it comes to making a major purchase, get help from professionals.

14

Imitation or Not?

Imagine a rosary-bead maker watching a fish being scaled in a basin of water. The water has colorful, pearly reflections which seem to form as the fish scales dissolve. The bead maker then gets the idea to filter the water, recover the pearly substance from it and mix it with a kind of varnish. Later he coats the inside surface of a hollow glass bead with the pearly mixture, fills the bead with wax, and what's the result? The birth of the modern-day imitation pearl.

This occurred in France in the 17th century. Jacquin was the name of the rosary-bead maker. And **essence of orient** (or **pearl essence**) is the name of the pearly mixture he discovered. Today, the finest imitation pearls usually have several coats of essence of orient.

Types of Imitation Pearls

Even though pearl essence is used to make many of the best imitation pearls, such as Majorica pearls, imitations come in a variety of types. The main ones are:

- **Hollow glass beads containing wax**. These pearls, made by the same process as Jacquin's, are most likely to be found in antique jewelry.

- **Solid glass beads**. Majorica imitation pearls are an example of this type. They may be covered with as many as forty coats of pearl essence and hand polished between each coat. Imitation glass pearls are also coated with other substances such as synthetic pearl essence, plastic, cellulose and lacquer.

- **Plastic beads**. These may have the same type coatings as the glass variety. Plastic imitation pearl necklaces sometimes hang poorly due to their light weight.

- **Mother-of-pearl shell beads.** These are coated with the same substances as plastic and glass imitations. A coating made from powdered mother of pearl and synthetic resin may also be used. One company calls such beads **semi-cultured**. This is just a misleading term for "imitation." Powdered mother-of-pearl coatings are not new. Centuries ago, American Indians produced imitation pearls by applying such coatings to clay beads and then baking them.

  Occasionally, people sell uncoated mother-of-pearl beads as pearls or they describe them as very valuable. In the Pacific Islands, you can buy mother-of-pearl shell bead necklaces from the natives for a couple of dollars. Some of the better ones cost more.

Simulated and **faux pearls** (the French term for fake pearls) are two other terms used to designate imitation pearls. These pearls can be distinguished from natural and cultured pearls with the tests that are described in the next two sections.

Tests that Require No Equipment Other Than a Magnifier

Tooth Test: Rub the pearls **lightly** along the biting edge of your upper front teeth. If they feel gritty or sandy, it's likely they are cultured or natural pearls. If they feel smooth, they are probably imitations.

There are a few problems with this test: it's not the most sanitary test; it may scratch the pearls if done improperly; and it doesn't always work. Some imitation pearls do feel gritty, and according to the Fall 1991 issue of *Gems & Gemology* (p. 176), real pearls may feel smooth. A cultured pearl sent to the GIA New York laboratory gave a smooth tooth test reaction because the surface had been polished. Therefore, don't rely solely on the tooth test. If you use it, combine it with the magnification tests listed below.

Surface Magnification: Examine the surface of the pearl with a 10-power magnifier such as a loupe. If it looks grainy, like a photo taken at an ISO of 1000 and above, there's a good chance it's an imitation (fig. 14.1). Pearls normally look unusually fine grained. Sometimes, though, dirt or pits on a pearl may make it seem to have a grainy appearance. Occasionally, too, freshwater and South Sea pearls may look a little grainy, but other surface characteristics mentioned in this section can prove they are not imitation.

If you have access to a microscope, also examine the surface at the highest possible magnification. At 50 power and above, a rough, pitted surface like the one in figure 14.2 means it's an imitation. Gas bubbles may also be present.

A surface with tiny, crooked lines giving it a scaly, maze-like appearance is characteristic of cultured and natural pearls (fig. 14.4). These scaly lines are not always evident at first. The surface may look smooth except for the flaws. Try using a strong, bare, direct light such as a fiberoptic and shine it on the pearl from various angles to find the scaly lines. It's curious that pearls, which feel gritty to the teeth, can look so smooth under high magnification whereas imitations, which feel smooth, tend to look coarse and rough. However, the less smooth an imitation is, the rougher it looks. On pearls, it's the "scaly-line" ridges that cause their gritty feel.

The best way to learn what the surface of pearls and imitations looks like under magnification is to examine many examples of each. When you can recognize how distinctive their surface textures are, you won't need to do any of the other tests to spot an imitation pearl.

Flaw Test: Examine the pearls for flaws. If they appear flawless, this is a sign they're imitation. Also note the types of flaws present. Many of those found on cultured pearls look different from those on imitations. If you examine pearl flaws with a 10-power magnifier whenever possible, it will be easier for you to recognize them. Chapter 6 shows examples of pearl flaws.

Matching Test: Note the shape, luster, size and color of the pearls. Imitations often seem perfectly matched, whereas there tend to be variations among the pearls on cultured or natural strands.

Heaviness Test: Bounce the pearls in your hand. If they feel unusually light, they're most likely made of plastic or filled with wax. Solid glass beads may feel heavier or about the same weight as cultured and natural pearls.

Fig. 14.1 Grainy surface texture of an imitation pearl viewed at 10-power magnification.

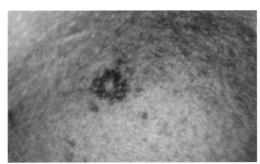

Fig. 14.2 Same imitation pearl at 64-power magnification. Note the rough surface.

ig **14.3** Under 10X magnification, the surface of he imitation pearl (top) looks coarse and grainy ompared to the smoother-looking surface of the eal cultured pearl (bottom). *Photo © R. Newman.*

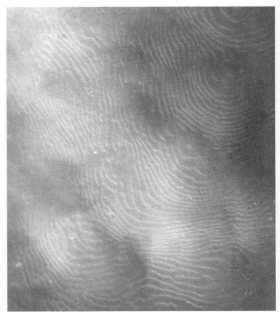

Fig. 14.4 Surface of a Tahitian cultured pearl viewed at 64-power magnification. The maze-like patterns prove the pearl is genuine. When rubbed lightly against the biting edge of the front teeth, the pearl feels gritty due to the microscopic surface ridges. *Photo © Renée Newman.*

Clasp Test: Is the clasp made of silver, steel or a gold plated metal. This is a sign that the strand may be imitation. Keep in mind, however, that good pearls are occasionally strung with cheap clasps and imitation ones with expensive clasps.

Price Test: Is the price of the pearls unbelievably low? If so, they may be imitation or have hardly any pearl nacre. Jewelers can't stay in business if they sell pearls below their cost.

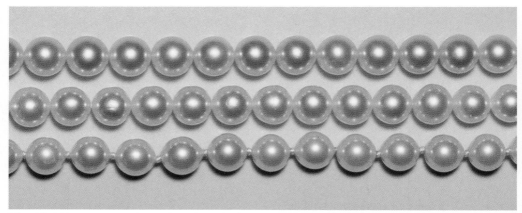

Fig. 14.5 Top two strands—cultured pearls, bottom strand—good-quality imitation pearls. Genuine pearls of good quality will typically have either pink, green, silver or blue overtones; whereas imitations tend to lack these overtones and be more uniform in color. A better way of distinguishing imitation from genuine pearls is to examine them with a 10-power magnifier. *Photo © Renée Newman.*

Overtone Test: Look for overtone colors in the pearls. Imitations frequently have none, and when they do, the overtones all tend to look the same. It's normal for cultured and natural pearls to have overtones, and these overtones often vary in color within the strand (fig. 14.5).

Drill Hole Test: Examine the drill hole area with a magnifier of 10-power or above. (On some pearls, it may be hard to see into their drill hole.) Cultured pearls tend to show the following characteristics (figs. 14.6–13.9):

- There is often a clear dividing line between the nacre and nucleus.
- The edges of the drill holes are often sharp and well defined. But when the nacre wears away it can leave the holes looking jagged and rough as in figures 13.8 and 13.9.
- The drill holes tend to be like a straight cylinder.
- The pearl nacre coating is normally thicker than the coating of imitations.

Imitation pearls tend to show these characteristics (figs 14.10 & 14.11):

- Typically, there is no dark dividing line between the coating and the rest of the pearl. Occasionally, one may see a kind of line, but the other characteristics of the drill hole will look like those of imitations. If you are in doubt, look at the drill hole opening on the other side of the pearl and on other pearls of the strand.
- The coating around the edges of the drill holes may have flaked off, making it look ragged or uneven.
- The drill holes may be angled outward at the surface of the pearl. Other times the drill holes may round inward at the surface and bow outward inside the pearl.
- The coating often looks like a thin coat of shiny paint. The thinness can be seen at the edge of the drill hole or around bare areas which expose the inner bead.
- Rounded ridges may have formed around the drill hole.
- If the bead is made of glass, its glassy luster may be apparent.

Drill Holes of Cultured Pearls

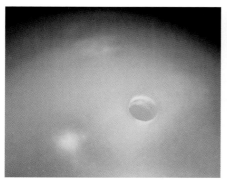

Fig. 14.6 Note the well-defined edges of the drill hole.

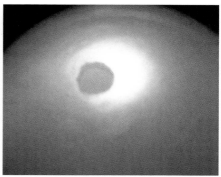

Fig. 14.7 A straight drill hole and the separation line between the core and thin nacre indicate this is a cultured pearl.

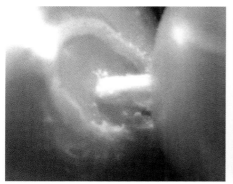

Fig. 14.8 The coating of both cultured and imitation pearls can wear way at the drill hole, but pearl nacre has a distinctive appearance and is usually thicker than that of imitations.

Fig. 14.9 The nacre has separated from the core in this pearl. A separation like this would not be characteristic of an imitation pearl.

Drill Holes of Imitation Pearls

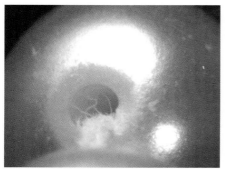

Fig. 14.10 The very thin ragged coating, angled-in drill hole, and lack of dividing line between core and coating indicate this is an imitation.

Fig. 14.11 Swirly formation around the drill hole and very thin glossy coating are clues this mother-of-pearl shell bead is an imitation.

Fig. 14.12 A $10 imitation 14-mm South Sea pearl necklace. Lack of overtone colors, flaked coating, swirly formations around drill-holes, and coarse surface texture under magnification are clues that this strand is fake. *Photo Renée Newman.*

Tests that Require Special Equipment

X-radiograph Test: An x-ray photo called an **x-radiograph** is taken of the pearls. Imitations are opaque to x-rays making them look solid white on the negative and solid black on the positive print made of it. Cultured and natural pearls are semitransparent to x-rays and usually look grayish.

Since imitation pearls can be positively identified with other tests, x-raying them usually is a waste of money. There is, however, a major advantage to the x-ray test. It's quicker to x-ray an entire strand at once than to test each pearl in it individually.

Refractometer Test: The pearl is placed on a refractometer (an instrument that measures a gem's **refractive index**—the degree to which light is bent as it passes through the gem). A pearl will generally have a low reading of 1.530 and a high one of 1.685. The numerical difference between these two readings is 0.155 and is called its **birefringence**. Pearls have an unusually high birefringence compared to other gems. This causes a blinking and pink effect when their refractive index is read through a rotating Polaroid filter. The GIA Pearls Course states that the presence of this "birefringent blink" is proof a pearl is not an imitation.

The refractive index of some imitations can also prove they are not cultured or natural pearls. For example, the Majorica imitation pearls the GIA tested for their Fall 1990 article in *Gems and Gemology* had a refractive index of 1.48, which was a conclusive means of identification.

Distinguishing between imitations and pearls is not difficult. Even lay people can learn how to detect imitations with a loupe, but they do need practice. It's more challenging to distinguish cultured pearls from those that are natural. That's the focus of the next chapter.

15
Natural or Cultured?

In 1917, the company Cartier bought its building in New York with two strands of natural pearls valued at a million dollars. In 1957, the pearls were sold at auction for $157,000. Perhaps one of the main reasons for this drop in price was the introduction of the cultured pearl, which decreased the demand for natural pearls.

Prices of natural pearls from oysters have risen considerably since 1957, and the concept of natural pearls has expanded to include any nacreous or non-nacreous natural pearls from any type of mollusk, including snails and clams. Some of these pearls were discussed and illustrated in Chapter 3. Additional photos have been added to this chapter.

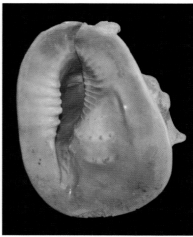

Fig. 15.1 Cassis paarls from the *Cassis cornuta* sea snail, which range in price from $200–$500 per carat wholesale. Cassis pearls are non-nacreous and found in the Indo-Pacific area. *Pearls from Pacific Coast Pearls; photo © Renée Newman.*

Fig. 15.2 *Cassis cornuta* or horned helmet shell from Pacific Coast Pearls. *Photo by David Rankin.*

Fig. 15.3 Penn (or pen) pearls form the *Atrina rigida,* a bivalve mollusk, which produces both nacreous and non-nacreous black pearls in the Americas. Non-nacreous penn pearls sell for less than $10 per carat and are drilled in India. Nacreous penn pearls wholesale from $50–$400 per carat. *Penn pearl necklace from Pacific Coast Pearls; photo: Gwendolyn Rankin.*

Fig. 15.4 Natural American freshwater pearl feathers and a gem studded cultured American fw pearl in a brooch by A & Z Pearls. *Photo by John Parrish.*

Fig. 15.5 Sea of Cortez tulip pearls in their *Modiolus americanus* (American horsemussel) shell. Prices of tulip pearls wholesale from $50–$500 per carat. *Pearls and shell from Pacific Coast Pearls; photo © Renée Newman.*

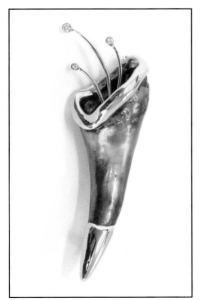

Fig. 15.6 New Zealand paua (abalone) pearl in a brooch by Moana Natural Pearl Co. *Photo by Rob Wright.*

Fig. 15.7 Scallop pearls in their *Nodipecten subnodosus* shell. They wholesale for $50–$1000 per carat and are found off of the coast of California. *Pearls and shell from Pacific Coast Pearls; photo © Renée Newman.*

Fig. 15.8 Mississippi River natural pearls from the private collection of John Latendresse. *Earrings by Paula Crevoshay; photo from Crevoshay Studio.*

Fig. 15.9 Natural conch pearl from the Sulu Sea in a ring handmade by Paula Crevoshay. Southeast Asian varieties of the Conch produce an extremely rare variety of white conch pearls. This white coloration is thought to be caused by the nutrients available to conchs in those waters, which may differ from nutrients in the Caribbean region. *Pearl from the collection of T. Stern; photo from Crevoshay Studio.*

Fig. 15.10 Natural saltwater pearls from the Persian Gulf and the coast of Central Asia (Oriental pearls). *Jewelry and photograph from the collection of K. C. Bell.*

Fig. 15.11 *Nautilus pompilius* pearl with a beautiful flame pattern. *Pearls from the T. Stern Collection; photo by Harold & Erica Van Pelt.*

Fig. 15.12 Giant clam (*Tridacna gigas*) pearl from *the T. Stern Collection; photo by J. Grahl – Courtesy: Société Des Perles Fínes.*

Fig. 15.13 Natural pearl from the *Pteria penguin* oyster. *Pearl from the T. Stern Collection; photo by J. Grahl – Courtesy: Société Des Perles Fínes.*

Fig. 15.14 Natural pearl from the *Pinctada maxima* oyster. *Pearl from the T. Stern Collection; photo by J. Grahl – Courtesy: Société Des Perles Fínes.*

Fig. 15.15 Natural 14-mm pearl (16.84 carats) from the Mississippi River. *Pearl from Pala Gems; photo by Wimon Manorotkul.*

Fig. 15.16 Melo melo pearl from the T. Stern Collection. *Photo by J. Grahl – Courtesy: Société Des Perles Fínes.*

Natural pearls are usually worth more than their cultured pearls counterparts; therefore, it's important to be able to distinguish between them. X-ray tests are typically required to prove a pearl is natural, but they are costly. Other tests can help you determine if a pearl is cultured and thereby save you the expense of an x-ray. These tests are listed below. Keep in mind that most of the pearls produced today are cultured. You are more likely to find natural oyster pearls in antique pieces since whole pearls were not cultured before the 1900's. However, the natural pearls in antique jewelry may have been replaced with cultured ones.

Tests a Layperson Can Do

Drill Hole Test: Look inside the drill hole with a 10-power loupe. If you can see **a dark dividing line separating the nacre from a pearl bead nucleus**, the pearl is cultured. This dark line is conchiolin, the material which binds the nacre to the bead. Natural pearls may show a series of growth lines, which get more yellow or brown toward the center of the pearl. A black deposit at the center of a white pearl can be a sign the pearl is natural (from *Gem Testing* by B. W. Anderson, p 219). Also note the **size of the drill hole.** The drill holes of natural pearls are rarely larger than .04 mm (.016 inch). Those of cultured pearls tend to measure .06 mm (.024 inch) (from *Pearls* by Jean Taburiaux, p 193). Natural pearls are partly valued by carat weight, so the holes are made as small as possible to minimize weight loss.

Shape Test: Do the pearls look perfectly round? If so, then it's likely they're cultured. Natural pearls tend to have at least slightly irregular shapes, even though a few are round. This test is only an indication; it is not proof.

Blink Test: Hold the strand near the front edge of a strong desk lamp. The light should shine through the pearls but not in your eyes. Rotate the strand. If the pearls blink from light to dark as they are turned, this indicates they are cultured and have a thin coating of nacre (imitation pearls with mother-of-pearl shell-bead centers may also blink). The dark areas result when there are dense mother-of-pearl layers on the shell bead which block the light. Figure 15.17 shows light and dark views of thin-nacre pearls with transmitted light. Cultured pearls with thin nacre may show only one view when rotated. In other words, they don't necessarily blink.

Stripe Test: As you rotate the pearls with strong light shining through them, look for curved lines and stripes (fig. 15.17). These are the growth layers of the shell beads. If they are visible, the nacre is very thin and the pearls are cultured. Not all shell bead nuclei show stripes, though. This can be seen in figure 15.18. Keep in mind that imitation pearls with shell-bead centers can also display this banded effect. Natural pearls, however, will not look striped.

Fig. 15.17 Dark and light views of thin-nacre pearls in transmitted light. Note the curved bands which indicate the growth layers of the shell bead nucleus. *Photo © Renée Newman.*

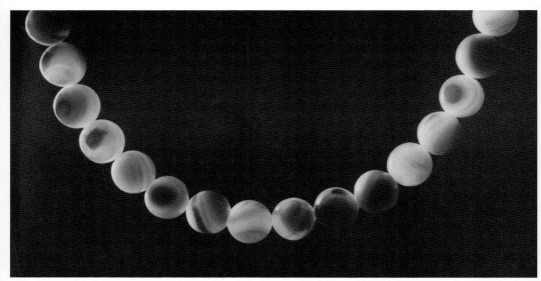

Fig. 15.18 Mother-of-pearl shell beads (the core of cultured pearls) seen with transmitted light. *Photo © Renée Newman.*

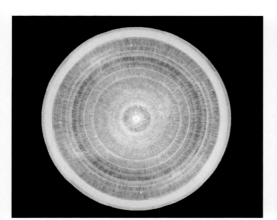

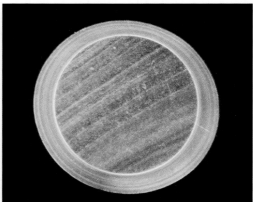

Fig. 15.19 Cross section of a natural pearl showing its concentric layers. *Photo © Gem-A, London.*

Fig. 15.20 Cross section of a cultured pearl. *Photo © Gem-A, London.*

Color Test: Examine the color. Cultured pearls often have a faint greenish tint, unlike natural pearls. Some dealers find that the color of natural pearls has a greater potential for brightness than that of cultured pearls. Color can only suggest a pearl might be cultured; again, it is not proof.

Matching Test: Because of their rarity, it's difficult to find natural pearls that match. Consequently, natural strands do not appear as well matched for color, shape, luster and size as those which are cultured.

Other Tests

X-radiograph Test: This is the most reliable way to distinguish between natural and cultured pearls. On an x-radiograph negative, cultured pearls usually show a clear separation between core and nacre. In addition, their core normally looks lighter than the nacre coating. X-rayed natural pearls tend to either present the same tone throughout or get darker in their center. A mantle tissue nucleus will look like a very dark, irregular-shaped void.

The disadvantage of x-ray tests is that it can cost between $100 and $300 to conduct them, and there are few gem labs that have the required equipment. Stephen J. Kennedy of the Gem Testing Laboratory of Great Britain provides good photos of x-radiographs in an article entitled "Pearl Identification" in the January-March 1998 issue of the Australian Gemmologist. This is also an excellent source of additional information on the identification of natural pearls.

X-ray CT: This detects the three-dimensional internal structure of a pearl by taking radiograms at various angles and reassembling the figures on a computer.

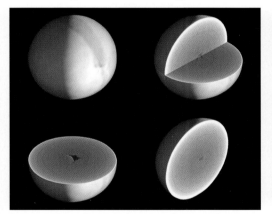

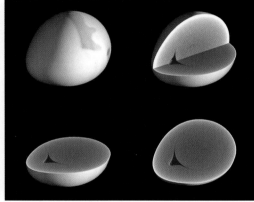

Fig. 15.21 CT 3D image photos of a non-nucleated freshwater cultured pearl courtesy of the GAAJ-Zenhokyo Laboratory.

Fig. 15.22 CT 3D image photos of a drop-shape bead-nucleated South Sea silver-lip pearl courtesy GAAJ-Zenhokyo Laboratory.

X-ray Fluorescence: This test is used in combination with an x-radiograph to provide the added information of whether the pearl is freshwater or saltwater. Natural saltwater pearls rarely fluoresce to x-rays. Freshwater pearls have a fairly strong yellowish x-ray fluorescence, whereas bead-nucleated saltwater pearls display a greenish fluorescence. Cultured pearls dyed with silver salts usually show no fluorescence.

Specific Gravity Test: The pearls are placed in a liquid that has a specific gravity of 2.71. (The liquid is purchased at gem instrument stores and tested with a piece of pure calcite.) The majority of natural pearls will float and others will sink slowly. Most cultured pearls with shell nuclei will sink quickly since they tend to be heavier than natural pearls. Black pearls show an SG of about 2.65. The biggest problem with this test is that the heavy liquid may damage the pearls, especially if the pearls are left in it too long. (See *Identification of Gemstones* by Michael O'Donoghue and Louise Joyner).

UV Fluorescence Test: The pearls are placed under long-wave ultraviolet light and compared to known samples of cultured and natural pearls. In his book *Gemstones* (p. 448), G. F. Herbert Smith mentions how cultured pearls can display a peculiar greenish fluorescence which differs markedly from the sky-blue effect of many natural pearls. He points out that this is not an infallible test because natural pearls can also have a greenish fluorescence, particularly if they are from waters adjacent to those of cultured pearls. Consequently, gem labs with x-ray equipment do not use this test. However, this test may help those without x-ray machines. Seeing a unique sky-blue fluorescence under LW UV light instead of a greenish-yellow glow may serve as an additional incentive to pay for an x-ray to test for natural origin. (This test is also mentioned in Webster' *Gems* on page 539.) Cultured pearl strands tend to show greater uniformity in the intensity of color.

Pearls from the *Pteria sterna* oyster have a distinctive red fluorescence, which distinguishes them from other dark pearls. An example is the Cortez Pearl® shown in figure 15.23.

If the pearls are of good quality and preliminary tests suggest they may be natural, then it's advisable to have them x-rayed. Appraisers and jewelers can send them to the appropriate labs for you. Some of the gem labs that have facilities to conduct x-ray tests are listed below. Jewelers or appraisers in your area may know of

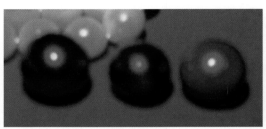

Fig. 15.23 Unique red LW fluorescence of a cultured saltwater Cortez® pearl on the right. A cultured Tahitian pearl is on the left and a natural Mexican black pearl from the *Pinctada mazatlan-ica* oyster is in the center. *Pearls from Columbia Gem House; photo by Douglas M. Moreno.*

others. For a list of independent appraisers and appraisal organizations, go to www.reneenewman.com and click on "appraisers."

Some Labs with X-ray Equipment for Pearl Testing

AIGS (Asian Institute of Gem Sciences), 919/1 Jewelry Trade Center, 33rd floor Bangrak, Bangkok, 10500, Thailand, (66-2) 267-4315- (66-2) 267-4320 www.aigsthailand.com

Central Gem Laboratory, 5-15-14 Ueno 5-Chome, Taito-ku, Tokyo 110-0005, Japan, Tel: (81) 3 (3836) 1627, www.cgl.co.jp

CISGEM, Via della Ordole, 4,1-20123, Milan, Italy, Tel: 39 02 8515 5230, www.cisgem.it

DSEF (German Gemmolgical Laboratory) Prof-Schlossmacher-Str. 1, D-55743 Idar-Oberstein, Germany 49 6781-43011, www.gemcertificate.com

GAAJ-Zenhokyo Laboratory, 8F Daiwa-Ueno Bldg., 5-25-11 Ueno, Taito-ku, Tokyo 110-0005, Japan Tel: +81-3-3835-2531, www.gaaj-zenhokyo.com

Fig. 15.24 Hand-executed Ceylonese gold neckpiece bead-set with natural pearls from Ceylon (Sri Lanka), early 19th century. *Necklace from the collection of K.C. Bell; photo by K.C. Bell.*

GIA Gem Trade Laboratory, Inc., 5345 Armada Drive, Carlsbad, CA 92008
Tel: (800) 421-7250 & (760) 603-4500, www.gia.org
   or
580 Fifth Ave., New York, NY 10036, Tel: (212) 221-5858

GIT (Gem & Jewelry Institute of Thailand), Chulalongkorn University,
Phayathai Road, Patumwan, Bangkok 10330 Thailand,
Tel: (662) 218-5470-4, www.git.or.th

Gubelin Gemmological Laboratory, Maihofstrasse 102,
6006 Lucerne, Switzerland, Tel: (41) (41) 26 17 17, www.gubelinlab.com

Laboratoire Française de Gemmologie, 2 Place de la Bourse
75002 Paris, France, Tel: 33- 1- 40262545, www.diamants.ccip.fr

SSEF Swiss Gemmological Institute, Falknerstrasse 9 CH-4001
Basel, Switzerland, Tel: (41) (6) 262-0640 Fax: 262-0641, www.ssef.ch

16
Antique & Estate Pearl Jewelry

A ntique dealers often describe their styles of jewelry with a period name based on the rule of monarchs or art movements. Many of the periods overlap, and the beginning and starting dates vary depending on the historical source. Before listing various jewelry periods, let's define some related terminology:

Antique jewelry: any jewelry one-hundred or more years old, as defined by the United States Customs Bureau. Webster's dictionary defines the term "antique" more loosely—any work of art or the like from an early period.

Heirloom, estate, or vintage jewelry: jewelry that has been previously owned by someone and that is typically passed on from one generation to another. It can range from a few decades to 100 or more years in age.

Collectibles: items gathered from a specific designer, manufacturer, or any period or periods in time. The items are collected according to the buyer's interests, and normally they are no longer in production, but they don't have to be as old as antiques. For example, Art Deco jewelry pieces are considered collectibles, but they are not true antiques—hence the phrase, "antiques and collectibles."

Figure 16.1 is an example of a true antique jewelry piece. Shown in its original presentation box, this necklace, dating to the 1800's, is part of a bridal parure presented to a Miss Wharton by her mother Constance in 1820. The Wharton family is known for Edith Wharton, the novelist, and the Wharton School of Economics.

The necklace consists of Oriental seed pearls painstakingly sewn with white horsehair onto shaped plaques of mother-of-pearl. Notable is the 13-inch length of the necklace: brides must have been smaller in those days.

Prior to 1893, all pearls were either natural or imitations. Seed pearls (tiny natural pearls) were the most plentiful, and were frequently used as borders encircling pendants and brooches. Freshwater pearls (river pearls) were also used in the 18th and 19th centuries.

Fig. 16.1 Early 1800's seed-pearl necklace acquired for the Pearl Society in Evanston, IL by Eve J. Alfillé in 1995. *Photo by Matt Arden.*

The first dark pearls from French Polynesia appeared on the market around the middle of the 19th century. They were not well accepted until the French Empress Eugenie made them fashionable around 1860. Natural black pearls from Mexico were also worn. Pearl prices were astronomical between 1893 and 1907, and accounted for more than 80 per cent of a jeweler's business. That is one reason why cultured pearls became so successful and predominated the 20th century. The culturing process made pearls more affordable for all social classes. The following pages illustrate some pearl jewelry from the 18th century up until about 1935.

Jewelry Eras Starting from the 18ᵗʰ Century until 1935

Georgian	1714–1837 (reigns of King George I – King George IV)
Victorian	1837–1901 (Queen Victoria 1837–1901)
Arts & Crafts:	1890–1914
Art Nouveau:	1890–1910
Edwardian:	1890–1915 (King Edward VII, 1901–1910) (Belle Epoque)
Art Deco:	1915–1935

Antique & Estate Pearl Jewelry

Fig. 16.2 Georgian natural pearl and diamond earrings, Skinner auction 3-18-2008, $15,998.00.

Fig. 16.3 Victorian natural pearl hat pin, Willian Doyle Galleries, 4-21-2009, $4,375.00.

Fig. 16.4 Victorian cultured pearl brooch-pendant. Weschler's auction, 4-25-2009, $645.25.

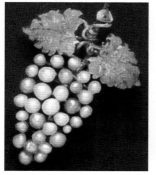

Fig. 16.5 Victorian seed pearl pin-pendant. Skinner 12-13-2005, $705.00.

Fig. 16.6 Victorian cultured pearl pin, Skinner, 3-17-2009, $7,703.00.

Fig. 16.7 Arts & Crafts, Tiffany & Co. cultured pearl brooch, Alderfer's auction, 4-20-2009, $4270.00.

Figs. 16.2–16.7 The photos of the antique pearl jewelry are from Gail Brett Levine's www.AuctionMarketResource.com, a comprehensive resource for antique to contemporary gems and jewelry auction sales data. On this website you can view thousands of items sold at jewelry auctions around the world and obtain gallery information, final prices, descriptions and gemological details of the pieces. The prices indicated are hammer prices, which include the buyer's premium.

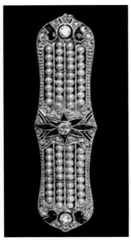

Fig. 16.8 Edwardian seed pearl brooch. Waddington's auction 12-04-2000, $1,533.33.

Fig. 16.9 Edwardian natural pearl necklace. Bonhams & Butterfield NY auction 4-16-2000, $1,220.

Fig. 16.10 Art Nouveau freshwater pearl brooch, Skinner auction 12-11-2007, $1,763.

Fig. 16.11 Art Nouveau cultured pearl brooch-pendant. Skinner 12-12-2000, $1,265.

Fig. 16.12 Art Deco natural pearl Jung & Flitz ring. Skinner, 3-17-2009, $8,295.00.

Fig. 16.13 Art Nouveau freshwater pearl brooch. William Doyle Galleries, 4-21-2009, $3,750.00.

Fig. 16.14 Art Deco natural pearl earrings. Sotheby's NY auction, 10-6-2004, $30,000.

Fig. 16.15 Art Deco conch pearl choker. Christie's NY 10-15-2003, $19,120.00.

Figs. 16.8–16.15 The photos of the antique pearl jewelry are from Gail Brett Levine's www.AuctionMarketResource.com, a comprehensive resource for antique to contemporary gems and jewelry auction sales data. On this website you can view thousands of items sold at jewelry auctions around the world and obtain gallery information, final prices, descriptions and gemological details of the pieces. The prices indicated are hammer prices, which include the buyer's premium.

Fig. 16.17 An American Arts and Crafts pin with natural Mississippi pearls in various shades of pink to purple. *Pin from the Pearl Society Collection; photo by Matthew Arden.*

Fig. 16.16 A Victorian pendant with natural half pearls, which were often used in Victorian jewelry. Half pearls were usually made by cutting off the best part of a hemispherical bright area(s) from a large irregular pearl. The side chain and large baroque freshwater pearl were added at a later date. *Necklace from Divina Pearls; photo: Cristina Gregory.*

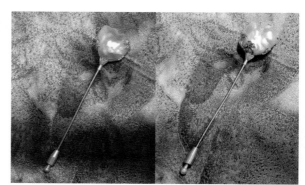

Fig. 16.18 Front and back views of a pin with a large heart-shape natural pearl decorated with platinum and diamond appliques probably added in the 19th century. *Pin from Pearl Society Collection; photo; Matthew Arden.*

17
Choosing the Clasp

M rs. Kirk was proud of the beautiful pearl necklace her daughter had given her, but she hardly ever wore it. She had arthritis, and that made it hard for her to fasten and undo the clasp. Since she lived by herself, nobody was around to help her put on the necklace, so it was easier to leave it in her jewelry box.

Mrs. Kirk is not alone. Complicated or hard-to-fasten clasps keep a lot of people from wearing some of their jewelry pieces. This could be prevented with a bit of forethought. When choosing a clasp, consider:

- How secure is it?
- How easy is it to open?
- How versatile is it?
- How much does it cost?

Determine what is most important to you about the clasp because normally some compromises will have to be made. For example, to get a clasp that is easy to open, you may have to accept less security.

Listed below are five basic pearl clasps along with their advantages and disadvantages.

- **Fish-hook clasp** (fig 17.1): This is a popular clasp because it's inexpensive and secure. It may be silver, gold or gold-plated. The main drawback of the fish-hook clasp is that it can be hard to fasten and undo, especially for someone with arthritis or other hand problems.

- **Push clasp** (fig. 17.2): The main advantage of this clasp, is that it is fairly easy to open, even with one hand when it's used on a bracelet. It's also relatively inexpensive. Unfortunately, it is not as secure as some of the other clasps.

- **Lobster clasp** or **lobster claw** (fig. 17.3). Secure, easy to open and relatively inexpensive, this is an ideal clasp both for pearls and gold chains. However, it's not used as frequently for pearls as the fish clasp and push clasp. If you're having pearls strung, you may wish to request this clasp.

Fig. 17.4 Magnetic clasp. *Photo © Renée Newman.*   **Fig. 17.5** View of magnetic clasp when closed. *Photo © Renée Newman.*

- **Magnetic clasp** (figs. 17.4 & 17.5). This is a good option for people with arthritic hands because it can be easily fastened and unfastened at the neck or wrist. However, it's not as secure as a lobster clasp or a clasp with a safety catch. Even though the magnets are strong, magnetic clasps are not recommended for heavy necklaces or necklaces with South Sea pearls or large, expensive gemstones. In most cases magnetic clasps can be worn with pacemakers, but it's best to consult your doctor first if you have a pacemaker. It's important to buy a good quality magnetic clasp; otherwise, the magnets might fall out. I own the clasp and pearls in figures 17.4 & 17.5. It has proven to be a secure, easy and convenient clasp, and I would buy another one. However, it took some practice to learn how to easily separate the magnets because they are so strong.

- **Screw clasp** (fig. 17.6): This clasp can add versatility when it's inserted in pearls to form a **hidden or mystery clasp**. For example, a long strand of pearls with three mystery clasps can be unscrewed and turned into a bracelet and two smaller necklaces.

Fig. 17.6 Mystery clasp

   Mystery clasps are fairly easy to open and close and are secure if they're screwed in all the way and aren't stripped out. They tend to cost a little more than the fish-hook, lobster and push clasps.

   Sometimes the string breaks on necklaces with mystery clasps. This can happen when people unscrew the clasp incorrectly or when they can't find the clasp and try to unscrew the necklace in a spot where there is no clasp. This problem can be avoided by having the jeweler show you how to find and open the clasp. When opening it, be sure to grasp at least two pearls on either side of the clasp. Turn them together as a unit. Don't twist the string.

There are a wide variety of clasps besides these four basic types. Figures 17.5 & 17.6 show a type of hinged clasp, the Applaudere by A & Z Pearls. Each end of the strand is attached to a clasp. The pair of clasps can be fastened over any of the pearls on the necklace allowing a variety of styles from a single strand of pearls.

Fig. 17.7 A hinged clasp, which is trademarked Applaudere by A & Z Pearls.

Fig. 17.8 Another view of the Applaudere clasp. *Photo by Richard Rubins.*

Fig. 17.9 Double ring clasp. *Pearl necklace and photo from Inter World Trading.*

Fig. 17.10 Push clasps set with sapphires, emeralds and pearls. *Photo and clasps from Inter World Trading.*

Fig 17.11 Bar clasp from Divina Pearls. *Photo by Crisitna Gregory.*

Fig. 17.12 Bar clasp from Divina Pearls. *Photo by Cristina Gregory..*

Another type of clasp is the double ring clasp with a thin opening that allows the rings to connect together (fig. 17.9). When necklaces or bracelets consist of multiple strands, bar clasps are commonly used (figs. 17.11–12). Many clasps are jewelry pieces by themselves and are best worn to the side or in the front of necklaces or on the top of bracelets. The next page shows decorative variations of the push clasp.

Fig. 17.13

Fig. 17.14

Fig. 17.15

Fig. 17.16

Fig. 17.17

Fig. 17.18

Fig. 17.19

Fig. 17.20

Figs. 17.9–17.20 An array of bracelet clasps from Divina Pearls. *Photos by Cristina Gregory.*

Fig. 17.21 Large baroque cultured pearls from Burma, Australia, China and the Philippines with an ammonite clasp. *Necklace design copyright by Eve J. Alfillé; photo by Matthew Arden.*

Fig. 17.22 Antique cameo centerplate and Tahitian cultured pearl necklace from Divina Pearls. *Photo by Cristina Gregory.*

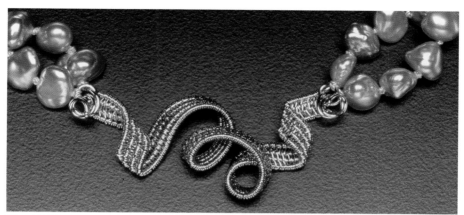

Fig. 17.23 A centerpiece hand woven by Barbara Berk and Chinese freshwater pearls. *Photo by Dana Davis.*

Sometimes accessories are used to accent pearls with plain clasps. One of the most popular pearl accessories is the **pearl enhancer**. It is a pendant which can be attached to a strand of pearls, as well as to a gold chain or bead necklace. The top of the pearl enhancer has a hinged clasp which closes over the necklace between two pearls (fig. 17.24). Centerpieces can be used to create impressive-looking necklaces (figs. 17.22 & 17.23).

Fig. 17.24 Reversible natural abalone pin/pendant/enhancer. *Design copyright by Eve J. Alfillé; photo by Matthew Arden.*

With the **pin pearl adaptor**, a pin can be attached to two strands to look like a decorative clasp or it can be worn as a pearl shortener (fig. 17.25). The pin pearl adaptor slides onto any pin and then can be closed over two strands of pearls.

There are many other types and styles of clasps besides the ones pictured in this chapter. You can see them on display in jewelry stores. No matter which type you choose, don't take a necklace or bracelet home without first having the salesperson show you how to fasten and unfasten the clasp.

Fig. 17.25 Pin pearl adapter

Under the salesperson's supervision, then try doing it at least two times by yourself. Some clasps are like puzzles, and if you try to figure them out on your own, you could damage the clasp and/or the pearls.

If your budget is limited, put your money into the pearls first, rather than into a fancy clasp. You can always upgrade the clasp later on. When buying a pearl necklace, your first priority should be the pearls.

18

Versatile Ways to Wear a Strand of Pearls

There are no other gems that offer more versatility than pearls. Queen Elizabeth I of England made the most of this feature. She wore yards of them as necklaces hanging down as far her knees. She had them threaded in her wigs, embroidered in her clothing, and set in her crown and other regal jewelry. You can also enjoy the versatility of pearls. The styles listed below can be made with just one opera-length necklace (about 28 to 34 inches) and a pair of hinged clasps like the Applaudere, pictured in the previous chapter.

- A single strand of adjustable lengths with the clasp in the back
- A double strand on one side and single on the other
- A double strand choker or princess necklace
- A single strand clasped to form one "chain" hanging in the front. An opera-length strand can be worn as a belt in the same manner.
- A single strand tied or knotted in front to form two "chains" hanging in the front
- Double strand in back and triple strand in the front
- A single strand looped in the front with a pearl shortener
- Double strand in front and single strand in back
- Double strand looped together in front
- Single strand with a clasp to the side or in the center
- Single strand knotted in the front. Dresses with low V-backs can be accented with a rope-length strand tied like this in the back.
- Double strand twisted and clasped in the back
- Double strand with a loop hanging in the front like a pendant
- Double or single strand with a pearl enhancer (detachable pendant)
- A closed double strand joined in the front with a solid surface pin. (This idea is from Joy's Antique Jewelry in Pittsburgh, PA.) (fig 18.1)
- Multi-strand bracelet
- Wrapped in the hair around a chignon or ponytail
- Attached to the side with a pin and hanging asymmetrically
- Pinned across a V-back dress or sweater

Fig. 18.1

Other options are possible with longer or multi-piece necklaces.

- Attached to the shoulders of a dress
- Wrapped around a hat
- Looped through buttonholes or openings in clothing

These are only some of the ways pearls can be worn. Use your imagination and you'll discover many more. Some examples are shown on the next pages.

Fig. 18.2

Fig. 18.3

Fig. 18.4

Three styles made possible with a 32 –36" strand of pearls and the oyster clasp from A & Z pearls. *Photos by Diamond Grapics; pearls & oyster clasp from A & Z pearls.*

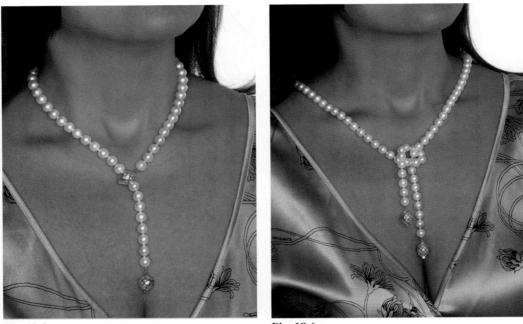

Fig. 18.5

Fig. 18.6

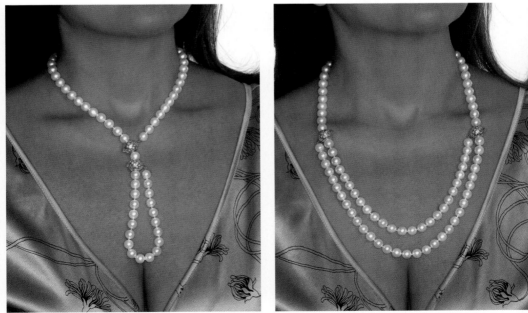

Fig. 18.7

Fig. 18.8

Four styles made possible with a 32 –36" strand of pearls and the oyster clasp from A & Z pearls. *Photos by Diamond Grapics; pearls & oyster clasp from A & Z pearls.*

Fig. 18.9 "Opposites attract" necklace created with Tahitian and freshwater pearls. Design copyright by Eve J. Alfillé. *Photo by Matthew Arden.*

Fig. 18.10 Pearls and photo from A & Z Pearls.

Fig. 18.11 Pearls from A & Z Pearls. *Photo by Renée Newman.*

Fig. 18.12 Photo courtesy Cultured Pearl Associations of America & Japan.

Fig. 18.13 Jewelry ensemble design copyright by Eve J. Alfillé. *Photo by E. Mariscal-Badami.*

19

Creating Unique Pearl Jewelry with Colored Gems

More and more designers are adding colored gems to their pearl jewelry. On the next few pages are some examples of how a variety of gems are being used to create innovative jewelry.

Fig. 19.1 Pin/clasp with carved black opal, freshwater pearls and South Sea pearl drop on a strand of South Sea pearls. *Carving, design, fabrication and photo by Angela Conty.*

Fig. 19.2 Necklace with matching earrings designed by Sandy Jones of Pearlworks. *Photo by Azad.*

Fig. 19.3 Wire-wrapped lavender spinel oval beads and pink Chinese freshwater pearl tassle. *Necklace by Sandy Jones of Pearlworks; photo by Azad.*

Fig. 19.4 Tourmaline and pearl pendant by Larry and Stacia Woods of Jewels by Woods. *Photo by John Parrish.*

Fig. 19.5 Natural color freshwater pearl earrings and tourmaline. *Earrings and photos from Eliko Pearl.*

Fig 19.6 Tahitian and Australian South Sea cultured pearls strung with aquamarine, morganite and green beryl. *Necklaces from King Plutarco; photo by Richard Rubins.*

Fig. 19.7 Aquamarine and keshi-type freshwater cultured pearls (also called reborn pearls or Zai Sheng Zhu in Mandarain). *Necklace from Yokoo Pearls Inc; photo from Inter World Trading.*

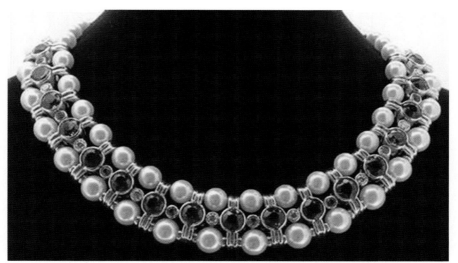

Fig. 19.8 Cultured pearl and amethyst necklace. *Photo and necklace from Albert Asher South Sea Pearl Co.*

Fig. 19.9 Rutilated quartz crystal beads intertwined with dyed and natural-color freshwater pearls. The necklace can be worn with the strands twisted or draped. *Photo and necklace by Betty Sue King of King's Ransom.*

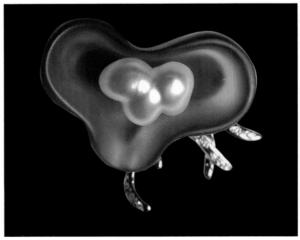

Fig. 19.10 South Seas cultured pearl in a "bowl" of smoky quartz carved by Dieter Lorenz. *Pin/pendant/ centerpiece design copyright by Eve J. Alfillé; photo by Matthew Arden.*

Fig. 19.11 Pearl and rubellite pearl enhancer by Anita Selinger. *Photo by Ralph Gabriner.*

Fig. 19.12 Fire opal and amethyst pearl enhancer. *Magic Pearl jewelry by Gabriele Weinmann; photo from Caricia Jewels Berlin.*

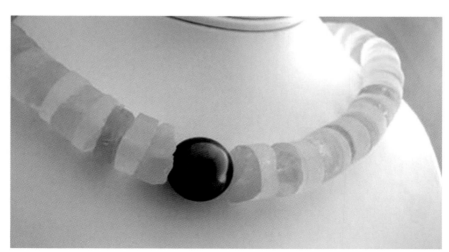

Fig. 19.13 Necklace from Kojima Company. *Photo by Sarah Canizzaro.*

Fig. 19.14 Natural conch pearl, sapphires and tsavorites in a handmade ring by Paula Crevoshay. *Photo from Crovoshay Studio.*

Fig. 19.15 Cortez™ Pearl and tourmaline earrings by Trigem Designs. *Photo from Columbia Gem House.*

Fig. 19.16 South Seas pearls and tourmalines. *Removable drops design copyright Eve J. Alfillé; photo by Matthew Arden.*

Fig. 19.17 Freshwater pearls embedded with opals in a butterfly created by A & Z Pearls. *Photo by John Parrish.*

Fig. 19.18 Pink sapphires and South Seas pearls. Jewelry from Divina Pearls. *Photo by C. Gregory.*

Fig. 19.19 Tahitian pearl ring and tourmalines from Kojima Company. *Photo by Sarah Canizzaro.*

Caring for Your Pearls

Which of the following is hardest and which is softest?

- A pearl
- An opal
- Pure gold
- A tooth

The hardest is the opal. It has a hardness of 5.5–6.5 on the Mohs scale, which rates the relative hardness of materials from 1 to 10. (The 10 rating of a diamond is the highest, but a diamond is over 1000 times harder than an opal.) **Hardness** is a material's resistance to scratching and abrasions.

The softest of the four materials above is pure gold, which has a hardness of 2–2.5. When alloyed with other metals, the hardness of gold increases, but it is still a relatively soft metal.

Tooth enamel has a hardness of 5, and a pearl has a range of 2.5– 4. In other words, a pearl is a relatively soft material.

Knowing how soft a pearl is can help us understand why pearls should not be tossed on top of or next to other gems in a jewelry box. Knowing that a tooth is harder than a pearl helps us understand why the "tooth test" for identifying imitations should only be done very lightly or else avoided. The basic concept of hardness is that a harder material will scratch one that is softer.

Besides being soft, pearls are easily damaged by chemicals or eaten away by acids such as vinegar and lemon juice. Heat can turn pearls brown or dry them out and make them crack.

One advantage of pearls is that, considering their softness, they are still fairly tough. In his book *Pearls*, Alexander Farn relates how jewelers and pearl merchants of old would separate imitation pearls from real ones by having footmen stomp on them. Those that were crushed were imitation. The natural pearls normally would resist such blows. Cultured pearls, especially those with thin nacre, are not this durable. Therefore, avoid dropping or crushing them.

Cleaning Your Pearls

The softness of pearls and their low resistance to heat and chemicals mean that special precautions must be taken when cleaning them. Keep in mind the following guidelines:

- Do not use commercial jewelry cleaners on pearls unless the labels say they are safe for pearls. Many of them contain ammonia, which will cause deterioration.

- Never clean pearls in an ultrasonic cleaner. It can damage the pearls and wash out the color if the pearls have been dyed.

- Never steam-clean pearls. Heat can harm them.

- Never use detergents, bleaches, powdered cleansers, baking soda or ammonia-based cleaners on pearls.

- Do not use toothbrushes, scouring pads or abrasive materials to clean pearls. They can scratch the pearls' surface. If there's a lump of dirt that can't be rubbed off with a soft cloth, try using your fingernails. They have a hardness of only 2 ½ or less.

Cleaning pearls is not complicated. After you wear them, just wipe them off with a soft cloth or chamois which can be dry or damp. This will prevent the dirt from accumulating and keep perspiration, which is slightly acidic, from eating away at the pearl nacre.

If the pearls have not been kept clean and are very dirty, they can be cleaned by your jeweler or they can be washed in water and a mild soap such as Ivory or Lux liquid. Note that some liquid soaps, such as Dawn, can damage pearls, so check to make sure the soap is mild enough before using. Clean the pearls with a soft cloth; pay attention to the areas around the drill holes where dirt may tend to collect. After washing the pearls, lay them flat in a moist kitchen towel to dry. After the towel is dry, the pearls should also be dry. Don't wear pearls when their string is wet; wet strings stretch and attract dirt which is hard to remove. Likewise do not hang pearls to dry.

Storing Your Pearls

Pearls are composed of about 2 to 4% water along with calcium carbonate and an organic binder called conchiolin. If the pearls become dehydrated, they can get brittle and crack. Consequently, they should not be kept near heaters or in places that get strong sunlight, such as on a window sill. Safe deposit boxes can be unusually dry, so if you ever store pearls there, try to take them out occasionally and expose them to humidity or moisture. Sealed plastic bags are not the best place for pearls either. The bags can keep them from breathing and getting moisture.

Since pearls are soft, they should be kept in something that will protect them from scratches. Jewelry pouches or cloth bags are ideal. Pearls can also be wrapped in soft material and kept wherever convenient. Jewelry boxes may be handy, but they are also the first place burglars look.

Having Your Pearls Strung

Pearl necklaces can stretch with time and the string can become dirty and weak. Thus, they should be restrung periodically—about once a year, but that depends on how often they are worn. Fine pearls should be strung with silk and with knots tied between each pearl. This prevents them from rubbing against each other and from scattering if the string should break.

Occasionally pearls are strung with gold beads. According to a Los Angeles pearl stringer, gold discolors pearls. Therefore, it's not advisable to string expensive pearls with gold beads.

Miscellaneous Tips

- Take your pearls off when applying cosmetics, hair sprays and perfume. These beauty aids are made of chemicals and acids which can harm your pearls.

- Take your pearls off when showering or swimming. It's not good to get the string wet, plus the chlorine or soap can damage the pearls. Pearl rings should be taken off when washing your hands or the dishes. Put the ring in a protective container or safe spot where it won't accidentally fall in the drain or get lost.

- When selecting pearl jewelry, check to see if the pearl is mounted securely. Preferably, the pearl will have been drilled and glued to a post on the mounting, especially if it is a ring. Otherwise, the pearl may come loose. If the pearl is flawless, a drill hole could lower its value. In such a case, it would be safer to set the undrilled pearl in a pin, pendant or earring than in a ring.

- When taking off a pearl ring, grasp the shank or metal part rather than the pearl. This will prevent the pearl from loosening and coming into contact with skin oil on your hand.

- Avoid wearing pearls with rough fabrics such as Shetland wool. They can scratch the pearls.

- About every six months, have a jewelry professional verify that the pearls on your jewelry are securely mounted or that the string is still good. Many jewelers will do this free of charge, and they'll be happy to answer your questions regarding the care of your jewelry.

Appendix

Chemical, Physical, & Optical Characteristics of Pearls

(The information below is mainly based on the following three sources:

Gems by Robert Webster
GIA Gem Reference Guide
Color Encyclopedia of Gemstones by Joel Arem

Chemical composition: $CaCO_3$ (most of it aragonite, the rest calcite) 82 to 92%
H_2O 2 to 4%
Conchiolin   4 to 14%
Other   about O.4%

Mohs hardness: 2.5 to 4.5

Specific gravity: White natural saltwater pearls: 2.66–2.76 except for some Australian pearls whose density may be as high as 2.78
Black natural saltwater pearls (Gulf of Calif:) 2.61–2.69
Conch pearls: 2.85
Natural freshwater pearls: 2.66–2.78
Japanese Akoya cultured pearls: 2.72–2.78 or more
Mantle-tissue nucleated cultured pearls: 2.67–2.70

Toughness: Usually good, but variable. Old, dehydrated, or excessively bleached pearls are not as tough.

Cleavage: None

Fracture: Uneven

Streak: White

Crystal character: An aggregate composed mostly of tiny orthorhombic (pseudo-hexagonal) aragonite crystals and sometimes hexagonal calcite crystals. Conchiolin, an organic binding material, is noncrystalline.

Optic Character: AGG, if not opaque (also listed as doubly refractive)

Refractive Index: 1.530–1.685

Birefringence: 0.155

Dispersion:	None
Luster:	Dull to almost metallic. Fractures may look pearly to dull.
Phenomena:	Orient. Varies from almost none to very noticeable.
Pleochroism:	None
Chelsea-filter reaction:	None
Absorption spectra:	Varies greatly, not diagnostic
Ultraviolet fluorescence:	None to strong light blue, yellow, green, or pink under both LW and SW. Natural color black pearls—none to moderate red to orangy red under LW; *Pteria sterna* pearls have a distinctive red fluorescence, which can be strong.
Reaction to heat:	Pearls can burn, split, crack, or turn brown in exces-sive heat such as an open flame. Prolonged heat may cause dehydration, which may cause nacre to crack..
Reaction to chemicals:	Attacked by all acids. Lotions, cosmetics, perspiration, and perfumes can also damage the nacre.
Stability to light:	Stable except for some dyed pearls.
Effect of irradiation:	Darkens color
Transparency to x-rays:	Semitransparent
X-ray fluorescence:	Natural saltwater pearls—inert except for a few white Australian pearls, which fluoresce faintly, cultured saltwater pearls—moderately strong to very weak greenish yellow depending on nacre thickness, freshwater pearls—moderate to strong yellowish white.
X-radiograph:	Cultured pearls usually show a clear separation between core and nacre, and their core normally looks lighter than the nacre coating. A mantle tissue nucleus will look like a very dark, irregularly shaped void. Natural pearls show a more or less concentric structure, and they tend to look the same tone throughout or get darker in the center.

Bibliography

Books and Booklets

Ahrens, Joan & Malloy, Ruth. *Hong Kong Gems & Jewelry*. Hong Kong: Delta Dragon, 1986.

Anderson, B. W. *Gem Testing*. Verplanck, NY: Emerson Books, 1985.

Arem, Joel. *Gems & Jewelry*. New York: Bantam, 1986.

Bauer, Dr. Max. *Precious Stones*. Rutland, Vermont & Tokyo: Charles E. Tuttle, 1969.

Bingham, Anne. *Buying Jewelry*. New York: McGraw Hill, 1989.

Blakemore, Kenneth. *The Retail Jeweller's Guide*. London: Butterworths, 1988.

Bloom, Stephen G. *Tears of Mermaids*. New York: St. Martin's Press. 2009.

Bruton, Eric, *Legendary Gems or Gems that Made History*. Radnor, PA: Chilton 1986.

Ciprani, Curzio & Borelli, Alessandro. *Simon & Schuster's Guide to Gems and Precious Stones*. New York: Simon and Schuster, 1986.

Dickenson, Joan Younger. *The Book of Pearls*. New York: Crown Publisher's, 1968.

Farn, Alexander E. *Pearls: Natural, Cultured and Imitation*. London: Butterworths, 1986.

Farrington, Oliver Cummings. *Gems and Gem Minerals*. Chicago: A. W. Mumford, 1903.

Federman, David & Bari, Hubert. *The Pink Pearl: A Natural Treasure of the Caribbean*. Milano, Skira Editore. 2007.

Federman, David & Hammid, Tino. *Consumer Guide to Colored Gemstones*. Shawnee Mission: Modern Jeweler, 1989.

Freeman, Michael. *Light*. New York: Amphoto, 1988.

Gemological Institute of America. *Gem Reference Guide*. Santa Monica, CA: GIA, 1988.

Gemological Institute of America. *The GIA Jeweler's Manual*. Santa Monica, CA: GIA, 1989.

Gemological Institute of America. *Proceedings of the International Gemological Symposium* 1991. GIA, 1992.

Greenbaum, Walter W. *The Gemstone Identifier*. New York: Prentice Hall Press, 1988.

Hall, Cally, *Gemstones*, Eyewitness Handbooks. London: Dorling Kindersley, 1994.

Idaka, Kimiko. *Pearls of the World*. Tokyo: Shinsoshoku Co., 1985.

Jackson, Carole. *Color Me Beautiful*. New York: Ballantine, 1985.

Japan Pearl Exporters' Association. *Cultured Pearls*. Japan Pearl Exporters' Association.

Jewelers of America. *The Gemstone Enhancement Manual*. New York: Jewelers of America, 1990.

Joyce, Kristin & Addison Shellei. *Pearls: Ornament & Obsession*. New York: Simon & Schuster, 1993.

Kunz, George Frederick. *The Curious Lore of Precious Stones*. New York: Bell, 1989.

Kunz, George & Stephenson, Charles. *The Book of the Pearl*. New York: Century Co., 1908.

Landman, Neil; Mikkelsen, Pula; Bieler, Rudiger; Bronson, Bennet. *Pearls: A Natural History*. New York: Harry N. Abrams, 2001.

Liddicoat, Richard T. *Handbook of Gem Identification*. Santa Monica, CA: GIA, 1993.

Lintilhac, Jean-Paul. *Black Pearls of Tahiti*. Papeete, Tahiti: Royal Tahitian Pearl Book, 1985.

Matlins, Antoinette L. & Bonanno, A. *The Pearl Book: 4th Edition*. South Woodstock, VT: Gemstone Press, 2008.

Marcum, David. *Fine Gems and Jewelry*. Homewood, IL: Dow Jones-Irwin, 1986.

Miguel, Jorge. *Jewelry, How to Create Your Image*. Dallas: Taylor Publishing, 1986.

Miller, Anna M. *Gems and Jewelry Appraising*. New York: Van Nostrand Reinhold Company, 1988.

Muller, Andy. *Pearls*. Kobe: Golay Buchel Japan, 1990.

Muller, Andy. *Cultured Pearls, the First Hundred Years*. Golay Buchel, 1997.

Nadelhoffer, Hans. *Cartier Jewels Extraordinary*. *New York: Harry Abrams, 1984*.

Nassau, Kurt. Gemstone Enhancement, Second Edition. London: Butterworths, 1994.

O'Donoghue, *Identifying Man-made Gems*. London: N.A.G. Press, 1983.

O'Donoghue, Michael & Joyner, Louise, *Identification of Gemstones*. Oxford: Butterworth-Heinemann, 2003

Powley, Tammy. *Making Designer Gemstone & Pearl Jewelry*. Glouster, MA: Rockport Publishers, 2003.

Preston, William S. *Guides for the Jewelry Industry*. New York: Jewelers Vigilance Committee, Inc., 1986.

Romero, Christie. *Warman's Jewelry*. Iola, WI: Krause Publications, 2002.

Rosenthal, Leonard. *The Pearl and I*. New York: Vantage Press, 1955.

Rosenthal, Leonard. *The Pearl Hunter*. New York: Henry Schuman, 1952.

Salomon, Paule. *The Magic of the Black Pearl*. Papeete, Tahiti: Tahiti Perles, 1986.

Schumann, Walter. *Gemstones of the World*. New York: Sterling, 1997.

Shirai, Shohei. *Pearls*. Okinawa, Marine Planning Co. Ltd., 1981.

Smith, G.F. Herbert. *Gemstones*. London: Pitman, 1949.

Strack, Elisabeth. *Pearls*. Stuttgart: Ruhle-Diebener-Verlag, 2006.

Taburiaux, Jean. *Pearls: Their origin, treatment and identification*. Radnor, PA: Chilton, 1985.

Ward, Fred. *Pearls*. Bethesda, MD: Gem Book Publishers, 2002.

Webster, Robert. *Gemmologists' Compendium*. New York: Van Nostrand Reinhold, 1979.

Webster, Robert. *Gems*. London: Butterworths, 1983.

Webster, Robert. *Practical Gemmology*. Ipswich, Suffolk: N. A. G. Press, 1976.

Periodicals

Auction Market Resource for Gems & Jewelry. P. O. Box 7683 Rego Park, NY. 11374.

Australian Gemmologist. Brisbane: Gemmological Association of Australia

Canadian Gemmologist. Toronto: Canadian Gemmological Association.

Colored Stone. Devon, PA: Colored Stone.

Gem & Jewelry News. Gemmmological Association and Gem Testing Laboratory of Great Britain.

Gems and Gemology. Santa Monica, CA: Gemological Institute of America.

The GemGuide. Glenview, IL: Gemworld International, Inc.

InColor. New York, ICA (International Colored Gemstone Association)

Jewelers Circular Keystone. New York: Reed Elsevier, Inc..

JQ Magazine. San Francisco, CA. GQ Publishing.

Jewelry Artist: Interweave Press

Jewelry Business. Richmond Hill, ON, Kennilworth Media, Inc.

Journal of Gemmology, London: Gemmological Association and Gem Testing Laboratory of Great Britain.

Modern Jeweler. Melville, NY: Cygnus Publishing, Inc.

National Jeweler. New York: National Business Media.

Palmieri's Auction/FMV Monitor. Pittsburgh, PA: GAA

Pearl World. Phoenix, AZ. Haggis House, Inc.

Rock & Gem. Ventura, CA: Miller Magazines, Inc.

Southern Jewelry News. Greensboro, NC, *Southern Jewelry News.*

Miscellaneous: Courses, Leaflets, etc.

A & Z Pearls Price List. Los Angeles, CA

"Cultured Pearls." The American Gem Society.

Gemological Institute of America Gem Identification Course. Santa Monica, CA.

Gemological Institute of America Colored Stones Course, 2002.

Gemological Institute of America Pearls Course, 1990.

Gemological Institute of America Pearl Description System Manual 2000

Gemological Institute of America Pearl Report folder with current grading definitions

"Grading and Information Guide." Midwest Gem Lab. Brookfield, Wi.

"Hints to select your cultured pearls." Rio Pearl. Hong Kong.

"I am a pearl." Mastoloni Pearls. New York, NY.

"Mastering Cultured Pearls." Adachi America Corporation. Los Angeles, CA.

"Pearl: Miracle of the Sea." American Gem Society.

"Pearl World." The International Pearling Journal. Haggis House, Inc., Phoenix, AZ.,

"Pearls of Japan." Japan Pearl Exporters' Association.

"Perle Noire: Quality comes first." Tahiti perles S C. Tahiti.

"Quality Cultured Pearls Price List." Adachi America. Los Angeles, CA.

"A Selling Guide for Retailers." Japan Pearl Exporters' Association.

"A Shopper's Guide to Cultured Pearls." J. C. Penney.

Shogun Trading Co. Price List. New York, NY.

Tara & Sons Inc. Price List. New York, NY

"Treasures from the Sea." Shogun Cultured Pearls. New York, NY.

"What you should know about cultured pearls." Jewelers' of America.

Index

Order Form

TITLE	Price Each	Quantity	Total
Pearl Buying Guide	$19.95		
Ruby, Sapphire & Emerald Buying Guide	$19.95		
Gemstone Buying Guide	$19.95		
Diamond Handbook	$19.95		
Exotic Gems, Volume I	$19.95		
Jewelry Handbook	$19.95		
Diamond Ring Buying Guide	$18.95		
Gem & Jewelry Pocket Guide	$11.95		
Osteoporosis Prevention	$15.95		
		Book Total	
SALES TAX for California residents only	**(book total x $.0825)**		
SHIPPING: USA: first book $3.00, each additional copy $2.00 Canada & Mexico - airmail: first book $12.00, ea. addl. $5.00 All other foreign countries - airmail: first book $14.50, ea. addl. $7.00			
TOTAL AMOUNT with tax (if applicable) and shipping (Pay foreign orders with an international money order or a check drawn on a U.S. bank.)		**TOTAL**	

Available at major book stores or by mail.

Mail check or money order in U.S. funds

To: International Jewelry Publications
P.O. Box 13384
Los Angeles, CA 90013-0384 USA

Ship to:

Name_____

Address_____

City_____ State or Province_____

Postal or Zip Code_____ Country_____

Other Books by RENÉE NEWMAN

Graduate Gemologist (GIA)

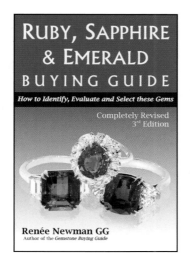

Ruby, Sapphire & Emerald Buying Guide

How to Identify, Evaluate & Select these Gems

An advanced, full-color guide to identifying and evaluating rubies, sapphires and emeralds including information on treatments, grading systems, geographic sources, lab reports, appraisals, and gem care. This 3rd edition has 173 new photos and two new chapters on geographic sources and appraisals versus lab reports. It updates gem professionals on recent treatments, jewelry styles, grading systems and geographic sources of rubies, sapphires and emeralds. Tips on detecting imitations and synthetic stones are also presented.

"**Enjoyable reading . . . profusely illustrated with color photographs** showing not only the beauty of finished jewelry but close-ups and magnification of details such as finish, flaws and fakes . . . Sophisticated enough for professionals to use . . . highly recommended . . . **Newman's guides are the ones to take along when shopping**." *Library Journal*

"**Solid, informative and comprehensive** . . . dissects each aspect of ruby and sapphire value in detail . . . a wealth of grading information . . . a definite thumbs-up!" C. R. Beesley, President, American Gemological Laboratories, *JCK Magazine*

"**A useful resource for both the experienced gemologist as well as the serious collector** . . . The book simplifies terms and explains concepts like cut, color treatments and lab reports clearly. The photographs, particularly in the sections of judging color, treatments, and clarity, are clear and true to life. All of the charts are clear and easily found and the book is well organized for quick reference. It is a handy, well organized and factually correct compilation of information with photographs that one will find themselves referencing on a regular basis." Kindra Lovejoy, GG, *The Jewelry Appraiser*

"**The best produced book on gemstones I have yet seen in this price range** (how is it done?). This is the book for anyone who buys, sells or studies gemstones. This style of book (and similar ones by the same author) is the only one I know which introduces actual trade conditions and successfully combines a good deal of gemmology with them . . . **Buy it, read it, keep it**." Michael O'Donoghue, *Journal of Gemmology*

187 pages, 280 photos, 267 in color, 6" by 9", US$19.95, ISBN 978-0929975412

Available at major bookstores and jewelry supply stores

For more information, see **www.reneenewman.com**

Other Books by RENÉE NEWMAN

Graduate Gemologist (GIA)

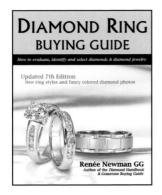

Diamond Ring Buying Guide

How to Evaluate, Identify and Select
Diamonds & Diamond Jewelry

"**An entire course on judging diamonds in 156 pages of well-organized information**. The photos are excellent . . . Clear and concise, it serves as a check-list for the purchase and mounting of a diamond . . . another fine update in a series of books that are useful to both the jewelry industry and consumers."
Gems & Gemology

"**A wealth of information** . . . delves into the intricacies of shape, carat weight, color, clarity, setting style, and cut—happily avoiding all industry jargon and keeping explanations streamlined enough so even the first-time diamond buyer can confidently choose a gem." *Booklist*

"Succinctly written in a step-by-step, outlined format with plenty of photographs to illustrate the salient points; it could help keep a lot of people out of trouble. Essentially, it is a **fact-filled text devoid of a lot of technical mumbo-jumbo.** This is a definite thumbs up!"

C. R. Beesley, President, American Gemological Laboratories

156 pages, 274 color & b/w photos, 7" X 9", ISBN 978-0-929975-40-5, US$18.95

Gem & Jewelry Pocket Guide

Small enough to use while shopping locally or abroad

"**Brilliantly planned, painstakingly researched, and beautifully produced** . . . this handy little book comes closer to covering all of the important bases than any similar guides have managed to do. From good descriptions of the most popular gem materials (plus gold and platinum), to jewelry craftsmanship, treatments, gem sources, appraisals, documentation, and even information about U.S. customs for foreign travelers—it is all here. I heartily endorse this wonderful pocket guide."
John S. White, former Curator of Gems & Minerals at the Smithsonian
Lapidary Journal

"**Short guides don't come better than this**. . . . As always with this author, the presentation is immaculate and each opening displays high-class pictures of gemstones and jewellery." *Journal of Gemmology*

156 pages, 108 color photos, 4½" by 7", ISBN 978-0929975-30-6, US$11.95

Available at major bookstores and jewelry supply stores

For more information, see **www.reneenewman.com**

Exotic Gems Volume 1

This is the first in a series of books that will explore the history, lore, evaluation, geographic sources, and identifying properties of lesser-known gems. *Exotic Gems, Volume 1* has 288 color photos of mounted and loose tanzanite, ammolite, zultanite, rhodochrosite, sunstone, moonstone, labradorite, spectrolite, andesine, amazonite, bytownite, orthoclase and oligoclase. Some of the pictures are close-up shots that show how to make visual judgments about clarity, transparency, color, cut quality and brilliance. A few pictures show how the gems are cut and many others show creative jewelry designs with these stones. *Exotic Gems* also provides tips on caring for the gems, selecting an appraiser and detecting imitations and gem treatments. The healing and metaphysical properties of the gems are also addressed. Written for both consumers and professionals, it's easy to read, well-organized, and packed with fascinating information and photos. If you're interested in colored gemstones, you'll find *Exotic Gems* to be a valuable resource that will help you discover and buy unusual gem varieties you may never have seen before.

154 pages, 288 color photos, 6" x 9", ISBN 978-0-929975-42-9, $19.95

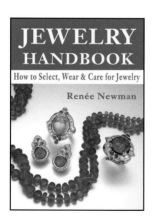

Jewelry Handbook
How to Select, Wear & Care for Jewelry

The *Jewelry Handbook* is like a Jewelry 101 course on the fundamentals of jewelry metals, settings, finishes, necklaces, chains, clasps, bracelets, rings, earrings, brooches, pins, clips, manufacturing methods and jewelry selection and care. It outlines the benefits and drawbacks of the various setting styles, mountings, chains, and metals such as gold, silver, platinum, palladium, titanium, stainless steel and tungsten. It also provides information and color photos on gemstones, birthstones, and fineness marks and helps you select versatile, durable jewelry that flatters your features.

"**A great introduction to jewellery** and should be required reading for all in the industry." Dr. Jack Ogden, CEO Gem-A (British Gemmological Association)

"**A user-friendly, beautifully illustrated guide,** allowing for quick reference to specific topics." *The Jewelry Appraiser*

"**Valuable advice for consumers and the trade**, specifically those in retail sales and perhaps even more for jewelry appraisers . . . An easy read and easy to find valuable lists and details." Richard Drucker GG, *Gem Market News*

177 pages, 297 color & 47 b/w photos, 6" x 9", ISBN 978-0-929975-38-2, $19.95 US

Other Books by RENÉE NEWMAN

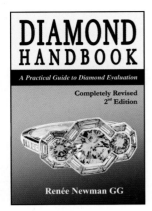

Diamond Handbook
A Practical Guide to Diamond Evaluation

Updates professionals on new developments in the diamond industry and provides advanced information on diamond grading, treatments, synthetic diamonds, fluorescence, and fancy colored diamonds. It also covers topics not in the *Diamond Ring Buying Guide* such as diamond grading reports, light performance, branded diamonds, diamond recutting, and antique diamond cuts and jewelry.

"Impressively comprehensive. . . . a practical, well-organized and concisely written volume, packed with valuable information. The *Diamond Handbook* is destined to become an indispensable reference for the consumer and trade professional alike."
Canadian Gemmologist

"The text covers everything the buyer needs to know, with useful comments on lighting and first-class images. No other text in current circulation discusses recutting and its possible effects ... **This is a must for anyone buying, testing or valuing a polished diamond and for students in many fields.**" *Journal of Gemmology*

186 pages, 320 photos (most in color), 6" x 9", ISBN 978-0-929975-39-9, $19.95

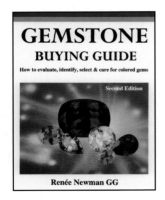

Gemstone Buying Guide
How to Evaluate, Identify and Select Colored Gems

"Praiseworthy, **a beautiful gem-pictorial reference** and a help to everyone in viewing colored stones as a gemologist or gem dealer would. . . . One of the finest collections of gem photographs I've ever seen ... If you see the book, you will probably purchase it on the spot."
Anglic Gemcutter

"**A quality Buying Guide** that is recommended for purchase to consumers, gemmologists and students of gemmology—irrespective of their standard of knowledge of gemmology. The information is comprehensive, factual, and well presented. Particularly noteworthy in this book are the quality colour photographs that have been carefully chosen to illustrate the text." *Australian Gemmologist*

"**Beautifully produced.** . . . With colour on almost every opening few could resist this book whether or not they were in the gem and jewellery trade."
Journal of Gemmology

156 pages, 281 color photos, 7" X 9", ISBN 978-0929975-34-4, US$19.95